All Loves Excelling

All Loves Excelling

Proclaiming Our Wesleyan Message

JOHN A. KNIGHT

Beacon Hill Press of Kansas City
Kansas City, Missouri

10   9   8   7   6   5   4   3   2   1

CONTENTS

PREFACE

It is a myth to assume that all of our pastors and people understand and can articulate fundamental Christian teachings, particularly those surrounding holiness and sanctification. Many can; some cannot.

Annually hundreds of men and women are ordained into the ministry of the church and assume pastoral responsibilities and other preaching and teaching assignments. While all of them have fulfilled the requirements of study and experience, significant numbers have received only minimal instruction and practice in the actual articulation of our distinctive doctrine of entire sanctification. These servants of the church deserve assistance in fulfilling their God-given charge.

Further, it is a joyous fact, but one filled with awesome implications, that a number equal to 60 percent of the total membership of the Church of the Nazarene have come into the fellowship of the Church in the last 10 years—over half a million *new* Nazarenes. Obviously the numbers for the past *two* decades are even more staggering. Our people must be instructed and discipled that they may know the resources for, and enjoy the thrill of, exemplifying Christ in all their daily relationships. They must be equipped to share with their friends and neighbors the "good news" of salvation and the personal fulfillment of a biblically based holy lifestyle.

This book has been prepared to assist in meeting this need. Much of the material incorporated in Part II of this volume was published earlier under the title *In His Likeness: God's Plan for a Holy People*. As a denomination-wide study book, it first appeared in 1976 and has been translated into several languages. Because of the warm reception it has received, the decision was made to represent it in a slightly altered and expanded form. The new title, *All Loves Excelling,* is taken from a sermon by the author originally printed in *Sanctify Them . . . That the World May Know* (1987) and published here in Part III as an example of a holiness expositional sermon.

Part I has been included to assist pastors and laypeople (i.e., Bible study leaders and Sunday School teachers) in fulfilling their responsibility to declare and clarify the biblical teaching of heart holiness and our *distinctive* doctrine of entire sanctification. Reproduced here in part, this first appeared in 1992 in the volume *Go . . . Preach: The Preaching Event in the '90s,* in a chapter called "The Holiness Pulpit: Our Wesleyan Message—Crisis and Process." In addition, selected ideas or excerpts are incorporated from *The Holiness Pilgrimage: Reflections on the Life of Holiness* (1973; Revised Edition, 1986).

These publications by the author are the property of Beacon Hill Press of Kansas City and Nazarene Publishing House and are printed together here in revised form by permission. The reader who wishes to discover additions, deletions, or other revisions is encouraged to acquire and refer to these earlier documents. Because this material is designed primarily to be a resource volume for pastors and Christian education teachers and workers, some duplications have been allowed and cross-referenced for emphasis.

The occasion for this distinctive presentation is to celebrate the 1995 Pastors' Leadership Conferences (PALCON IV). If pastors and people through these materials are inspired and challenged and empowered to depict and dramatize—in ways that are relevant and attractive—the possibilities of holy living in Christ through the indwelling Holy Spirit, the purpose of this volume will be accomplished "to the glory of God the Father."

JOHN A. KNIGHT, M.A., B.D., Ph.D.

TO PREACH HOLINESS
OR
NOT TO PREACH HOLINESS
(That Is the Question)
"Called to Be Holy"
1 COR. 1:2, NIV

"Holiness is a *doctrine* to be believed,
an *experience* to be enjoyed,
and a *life* to be lived."

—J. B. CHAPMAN
(Holiness—
the Heart of Christian Experience)

1

Our Holy Call

The admonition to preach holiness, or any discussion of it, may foster the impression of a misplaced or unbalanced emphasis. Some may infer erroneously that the call to preach holiness is an appeal to preach at best a fragment of the gospel or at worst a narrow theological provincialism. To avoid these unjustified perceptions, one must consider the topic in a broad and comprehensive context.

Preach the Gospel of Christ

Paul explicitly states what the heart of the preacher's message should be. To the Corinthians he insisted: "Christ did not send me to baptize, but to preach the gospel—not with words of human wisdom, lest the cross of Christ be emptied of its power" (1 Cor. 1:17, NIV).

The preacher is commissioned to preach the gospel. However, the gospel is a Person, not a creed or doctrine. The gospel is a Person, not a ritual. The gospel is a Person, not a book (not even the Bible). Christ does not *have* the gospel, nor preach it merely. He *is* the gospel. He *is* the "good news."

Our message is not a principle, nor a perspective, but a Person. Thus Oswald Chambers observed, "We are nowhere told to preach salvation, or sanctification, or Divine Healing; we are to lift up Jesus, who is the Redeemer, and He will produce His redemptive results in the souls of men."[1] Even more explicitly he admonished: "Don't preach salvation; don't preach holiness; don't preach the baptism of the Holy Ghost; preach Jesus Christ and everything else will take its rightful place."[2]

When any doctrine is preached in place of Christ, or apart from Him and His redemptive action on the Cross, the message becomes sterile, powerless, and dull. When He is exalted the message is alive, powerful, and fruitful because He promised: "And I, if I be lifted up from the earth, will draw all men unto me" (John 12:32).

The heart of our message must be Christ Jesus. Paul lifted up the exalted title of "Christ," and then added, *"whom we preach"* (Col. 1:28, italics mine throughout). Not "what," mind you, but "whom." Anointed preaching is more than stating a valid position, or propagating a distinctive doctrine, or proclaiming truth *about* Christ. It is Christ himself being ministered to people in the power of the Spirit.

Our preaching must not merely assume Christ. It must be explicitly Christ-centered—the preexistent Christ, the incarnate Christ, the sinless Christ, the atoning Christ, the resurrected Christ. *It must focus on the Christ who baptizes with the Holy Spirit,* the Christ who is Lord of His Church, and the Christ who will return to catch away His waiting Bride.

Preach Holiness—the Demand of Christ

To say all this in no way obviates the necessity of the preacher to preach holiness. If our task is to preach the gospel who is Christ, one pervasive aspect of that gospel is the requirement and possibility of holiness and holy living; that is, being like Christ.

The social problems of our day clamor for solutions that the message of holiness provides. Nothing is more relevant than holiness to the social epidemics that surge through our times—crime, divorce, delinquency, child abuse, guilt that produces all kinds of psychological disturbances, dishonesty in government and in the workplace, lack of integrity, intemperance, racial and international conflict.

Richard Taylor has correctly stated: "Apart from heart holiness, the political, social, and international sores may be anointed with man-made salves and be bound with man-made bandages, but they cannot be healed. The world can manufacture crutches for a crippled race but it takes the holiness preacher to show the way to perfect soundness and wholeness."[3]

Apart from the enabling Spirit of Christ, the church will be powerless in its attacks on Satan and his cohorts. Thus the church needs a renewed emphasis on the preaching of holiness, both for its own sake and in order "that the world may know" (John 17:23).

The church cannot meet the challenges of the 1990s and of the 21st century apart from its embodiment and declaration of holiness, which is the Spirit of Christ. We must make known God's answer to current dilemmas, and God's answer is Christ. E. Stanley Jones pointed out that Christ's answer is the Kingdom centered around the cleansing and empowering Holy Spirit.[4]

If the "times demand it," "the church needs it," and "the gospel requires it," as Richard Taylor has suggested,[5] then we as preachers have no choice but to proclaim deliverance from sin, both outward and inward, through Christ.

Our Continuing Assignment—to Preach Holiness and Entire Sanctification

We believe God has raised up the Church of the Nazarene to bear witness to "entire sanctification." Our primary reason for existence is to assure men and women that "the blood of Jesus Christ . . . cleanseth . . . from *all* sin" (1 John 1:7).

Our *central* and *cardinal* doctrine is *redemption*, or salvation, through Christ. This is in harmony with Paul's words: "For I delivered to you as of *first importance* what I also received, that Christ *died for our sins* . . . , that he was buried, that he was raised on the third day in accordance with the scriptures" (1 Cor. 15:3-4, RSV).

This redemption is *totally* adequate to meet humankind's deepest spiritual need. The atonement of Christ when appropriated by repentance and faith, and/or consecration and faith, not only nullifies the *works* and manifestations of sin—that is, sins and sinning—but the *condition* of sin itself, the *in-being* or inner sin. The salvation of Christ deals both with the *symptoms* of sin and with the *disease* itself.

Such a glorious gospel needs to be declared in all its fullness. Could it be that the original impetus that brought us as a movement into existence, namely, to spread "scriptural holiness over these lands," is being dissipated by neglect or silence? There is little danger that our doctrinal position will be altered in our official creedal affirmations. There is great peril, however, in the tendency to "overlook" or ignore our doctrinal distinctives while their clear statement in the *Manual* goes unchanged but unnoticed. One religious historian has stated our danger: "Beliefs seldom become *doubts;* they become *ritual.*"[6]

Perhaps there are pastors who do not preach holiness because they feel unprepared to do so. The late General Superintendent G. B. Williamson has framed an appropriate response to this feeling of inadequacy: "It is the duty of all who are chosen to preach holiness to qualify themselves for such a high calling."[7] A primary prerequisite for such qualification is to be persuaded in one's own mind that our doctrinal position is in harmony with the Scriptures. Further, one should understand the fundamental ideas associated with this teaching and assure oneself of its philosophical and psychological soundness.

These advantages, which arise from careful and prayerful study, are not desirable for the sake of debating the issue nor for formulating a defense against opposing views. Rather, they are valuable because they provide the preacher with conviction and authority. A preacher of holiness must know more than the theoretical basis of the doctrine—an experiential encounter with the reality of sanctification is required.

| 2 |

Preaching with Understanding

Holiness is not an optional theme or emphasis within the Christian faith. Rather, it is the Christian faith itself. One cannot proclaim the gospel without simultaneously preaching holiness, which as John Wesley put it, is "loving God with all one's heart, soul, mind, and strength, and one's neighbor as oneself."[1]

People do not oppose or reject our holiness message because they think it is an isolated theme or fringe idea that is separated from the gospel unless we have, through faulty preaching and teaching, led them to that erroneous conclusion. Rather, they reject it because they have misconceptions as to what holiness is—or because they are not willing to yield to the claims of Christ and the gospel.

Our assignment as preachers is to replace these misconceptions with sound biblical teachings; and to affirm the scriptural demand for radical commitment and obedience and for cleansing of the heart through Christ's baptism in the Spirit, which we know as "entire sanctification."

If the preacher understands the gospel and the message of holiness, he or she will understand that preaching it is an imperative. A true Christian preacher will preach holiness. Nazarene preachers, I believe, are anxious to declare "the whole counsel of God."

As a result, this chapter is not concerned with methodologies or techniques of preaching, but rather with key ideas that are fundamental to understanding our message of holiness. My prayer is that the Holy Spirit will illuminate our minds and kindle a fire within us to proclaim for Christ's glory our cardinal doctrine of holiness (holy living) and our *distinctive* doctrine of entire sanctification. And, further, acknowledging the critical need for adequate clarification, that we will not be fearful of using this terminology—while investing it with fresh explanation and definition.

Holiness and Entire Sanctification

Is holiness being preached to our people? I believe the answer is "Not as clearly or effectively as it should be." Sometimes preachers ask, "How often should one preach holiness?" The question in this form may arise out of shallow understanding of what holiness and holiness preaching is.

Are we talking about "holiness" or "entire sanctification"? Generally if preachers indicate that they preach our distinctive doctrine every time they preach, they are talking about "holiness." Others may indicate they preach it once a month or once a quarter. More than likely they are thinking of "entire sanctification."

The terms *holiness* and *sanctification* have similar meanings and are often used interchangeably in our extemporaneous preaching. However, there are important shades of meaning that distinguish them, which if understood can avoid a variety of pitfalls.

Sanctification is that act and/or process of God's grace by which one is made "holy." *Holiness* is that quality of life that follows from "sanctification" or from "being sanctified." *Sanctification,* then, is the means to holiness or holy living. (See Part II, p. 89.)

Sanctification in its broadest sense, resulting in holiness or holy living, is a *process* of moral and spiritual renewal beginning with *regeneration* and continuing throughout the Christian life to final *glorification*.

We believe, however, that Christ's atonement provides more than is experienced in this early stage of salvation or initial sanctification. We also affirm that within the process of the believer's renewal in the image of God there is a distinct or identifiable moment when the believer is, or can be, cleansed from the in-being sin, that is, the inner condition of sinfulness. This distinctive work of grace we call *entire sanctification* as distinct from *initial sanctification*.

Entire sanctification is sometimes referred to as a *crisis* experience. The word is not intended to connote an emergency in one's Christian walk, but rather an act of God that takes place in a moment of consecration and faith. (See Part II, p. 108.) This second work of grace is, or may be, as distinct and dramatic as the first work of regeneration—or even more so.

We have noted earlier that we are to preach Christ, who *is* the gospel. This gospel mandates holiness, which is the design of God's self-revelation in Jesus Christ. Holy living is the end toward which God is working in the lives of all people everywhere. Thus the Scriptures teach that:

- God has chosen us "before the foundation of the world . . . that we should be holy" (Eph. 1:4).
- God chastens or disciplines His children that they "might be partakers of his holiness" (Heb. 12:10).
- The Word, the Truth, Jesus Christ himself, is the instrument of our sanctification and holiness (John 17:17).
- Christ gave himself for us to redeem us from *all* iniquity and "purify for himself a people that are his very own, eager to do what is good" (Titus 2:14, NIV).

- The Holy Spirit is given to sanctify—"God hath from the beginning chosen you to salvation through sanctification of the Spirit and belief of the truth" (2 Thess. 2:13). "Not by works of righteousness which we have done, but . . . by the washing of regeneration, and renewing of the Holy Ghost" (Titus 3:5).

In short, holiness is *salvation!* To be converted to Christ is to be set on the road to moral and spiritual perfection, to a life of holiness. We reiterate: Holiness is begun in regeneration and will be completed only with our glorification at the last day.

Within this continuum that is the believer's pilgrimage, there are two distinctive and identifiable moments, which we know respectively as conversion and entire sanctification. Conversion is God's solution to man's guilt, and it brings forgiveness of sins. Conversion is God's solution to man's death, and it brings life and new birth. Conversion is God's solution to man's alienation and estrangement, and it brings reconciliation and adoption into the family of God. (See Part II, p. 122.)

Entire sanctification is God's answer to man's fundamental pollution of sin, sin in embryo, the being of sin, the spirit of self-sovereignty, the fountain and condition of sin; and it brings cleansing as well as the coherence and integrity of the self.

Salvation as Deliverance from Sin

Salvation in its broadest sense includes the beginning of saving grace and extends to our deliverance from evil effects of this present world. We may speak of it as a past event, a present experience, and a future hope. In referring to salvation, the Scriptures employ all three verb tenses:

1. In relation to the *past*, we "have been saved" (Eph. 2:8, RSV; also 2 Tim. 1:9 and Titus 3:5, RSV).

2. In relation to the *present,* we "are being saved" (1 Cor. 1:18, RSV; also 2 Cor. 2:15, RSV).
3. In relation to the *future,* "we shall be saved" (Rom. 5:10; 10:13; 11:26; also Matt. 10:22; Acts 15:11; 1 Tim. 2:15).

Hence there is biblical justification for the distinction in holiness theology between initial salvation in justification and regeneration (which occur in the moment of conversion), full salvation in entire sanctification, continuous salvation in maturation and growth by grace, and final salvation in glorification.

Salvation means "deliverance" from sin. Thus holiness preaching is correct when it affirms that in justification we are delivered from the *penalty* and *guilt* of sin. Simultaneously in regeneration we are delivered from the *power* and *dominion* of sin. In entire sanctification we are delivered from the *pollution* or *corruption* of sin. In glorification, when we have a resurrected body, we shall be delivered from the *presence* and *effects* of sin.

At every stage we are being delivered or saved continuously, moment by moment by the grace of God expressed in Christ's atoning work in our behalf apprehended by faith. (See Part II, p. 126.)

Believers sometimes testify that they "are saved and sanctified," thus identifying the two major works of grace, namely, conversion and entire sanctification. They mean that they have been saved and subsequently sanctified. The definite quality of such testimonies is much to be desired.

Preachers who seek to communicate our distinctive doctrine need to know, however, that such popular holiness terminology is not altogether biblical. The truth is that one is also sanctified *initially* when first saved and is *being saved* when one is entirely sanctified. It might be more in accord with scriptural usage to say that one is not saved until he is sanctified *wholly.* Wesley referred to these as *"true believers."* But even this is not the complete picture, since one will not be *finally* saved until the last day when one makes that abundant entrance into the heavenly Kingdom.

Stages of Salvation

Holiness is that quality of life that results from being saved through the process and/or act of sanctification. There are, therefore, degrees of holiness and degrees or stages of salvation. Such an understanding is imperative for the biblical preaching of holiness. John Fletcher, saintly contemporary of John Wesley, pointed out in his *Portrait of St. Paul* that if preachers are to be effective communicators of holiness, they must understand the stages of salvation and must know the stages in which their hearers are living.

When we talk about "preaching holiness," we can have in mind one of two concepts that are related but different: (1) the moment of entire sanctification, or (2) the life of holiness, which involves our relationships to God, people, and things. There have been periods in the Holiness Movement when one or the other of these emphases has been neglected. When that occurs, we pay dearly because the spiritual development of countless persons is stunted, or self-righteousness replaces total dependence on Christ.

Emphasis on the first is necessary in order to underscore the truth that entire sanctification comes by faith and in an instant. Salvation is by grace through faith. On the other hand, to limit our preaching only to the crisis of entire sanctification is to interpret holiness too narrowly. Often this binds our preaching to little more than a perennial exhortation to a certain preconceived "experience," to a kind of "one size fits all" spiritual straitjacket. If there is nothing more, methodology is overstressed, and the moral and life-related aspects of the holy life are obscured. This is something less than true holiness preaching.

Emphasis on the second concept apart from the first leaves the believer with the impression that one can "grow" into holiness. An insidious corollary is the notion that our works over a period of time can bring about this development. Further, it keeps the believer constantly in doubt as to where one is in one's spiritual journey. A constant feeling of one's "spiritual pulse" is the result, along with a gnawing fear that one has not done enough to gain God's favor. Keeping the "law" may become more important than maintaining a right relationship with God. Self-righteousness, which is the opposite of the gospel, shrivels the soul.

Mildred Wynkoop describes this consequence powerfully: "When the dynamic of holiness theology wanes, its ideals tend to be translated into a moralism which isolates people from the life in which they need most to be immersed. Moralism ends in spiritual bankruptcy."[2]

True holiness preaching deals deliberately and thoroughly with both *crisis* and *process*. This is done best when the full-orbed gospel of Christ is preached. Wynkoop continues:

> Only the spiritual and moral approach characteristic of the New Testament message continues to throb with life century after century, and—more miraculously—throughout the expanding life of a person. The true holiness message does not exhaust itself in issues which are discarded by a growing psyche. Maturity cannot outdate it. Properly preached, "holiness" has no ceiling. It is as big as the future and more challenging than the deepest capacity any human person can possibly fully explore.[3]

Holiness preaching that is biblical relates the moral imperative to human experience. It presents the claims of

Christ upon every facet of the personality and its relationships.

The preacher of holiness must remember that although the Spirit sometimes convicts of something unethical, the primary work of the Holy Spirit is to reveal that which dethrones the Lord Jesus in the life and keeps Him from being sovereign Lord over all.

The preacher of holiness, therefore, knows that his task is not to convict another for sin, not even the inbred sin that lies deep in the human heart. The Spirit, however, uses holiness preaching to convict even the unconverted. Whoever the audience may be—unconverted or believer who is yet not sanctified "wholly"—according to Wesley, we should preach it "always by way of promise; always drawing, rather than driving."[4]

The Church of the Nazarene has distinguished itself by bringing believers into that stage of holiness described by the phrase "sanctified wholly." Wesley called such persons "altogether Christians" and "fathers in Christ." Fletcher taught that such persons have their spiritual existence in the "dispensation of the Holy Spirit."

Our distinctive doctrine that describes this stage of holiness is stated in Article X of the Articles of Faith in the Nazarene *Manual* (italics mine):

> We believe that entire sanctification is that *act of God, subsequent to regeneration,* by which believers are *made free* from original sin, or depravity, and brought into a state of *entire devotement to God,* and the holy *obedience of love* made perfect.
>
> It is wrought by the baptism with the Holy Spirit, and comprehends in one experience the *cleansing of the heart from sin* and the *abiding, indwelling presence of the Holy Spirit, empowering the believer for life and service.*
>
> Entire sanctification is *provided by the blood of Jesus,*

is wrought *instantaneously by faith,* preceded by *entire consecration;* and to this work and state of grace *the Holy Spirit bears witness.*

This experience is also known by various terms representing its different phases, such as "Christian perfection," "perfect love," "heart purity," "the baptism with the Holy Spirit," "the fullness of the blessing," and "Christian holiness."[5]

The key affirmation as indicated by the italics may be stated as follows: Entire sanctification is a divine work that instantaneously by faith brings: *(a)* freedom or cleansing from original sin (the spirit of sin); *(b)* assurance through the abiding presence of the Holy Spirit who empowers for service; and *(c)* entire devotement to God.

These ideas can be preached clearly in a single message, or, preferably, in a series of sermons. We should assume that our hearers either accept our doctrine of holiness and entire sanctification or will do so if convinced on the basis of Scripture. Consequently, our preaching must be biblical, and we must strive for clarity and understanding.

The preacher, especially the preacher of holiness and entire sanctification, not only must preach so as to be understood but also must preach so as *not to be misunderstood.* The preacher must overcome certain misconceptions and faulty assumptions held by the hearers. These misconceptions or assumptions may hinder the believer from entering the "fullness of the blessing" or from leading others into the "more perfect way."[6]

Clarifying Our Message—Biblically, Theologically, Psychologically, Ethically

Every preacher of holiness and entire sanctification should know John Wesley's list of 30 favorite biblical texts on holiness and sanctification.[7] They do not all demonstrate secondness clearly, but they do describe the character of the entirely sanctified person.

We believe that entire sanctification deals a deathblow to what we have called "depravity" or self-centeredness. However, in clarifying our message *biblically,* we as preachers must seek to avoid clichés and terms that may cause problems in understanding. For example, if *eradication* is misleading to some, the truth can be preserved—as it should be—by using biblical terms such as *crucifixion* or *mortification.* The biblical writers used strong and decisive words like *purge, purify, remove dross, eliminate, annul, abolish, put an end to, dissolve, melt, crucify, break up, put off, mortify, kill,* or *render extinct.* (See Rom. 6:6, 11; Col. 2:11; see also Part II, p. 114.)

Further, to preach holiness and entire sanctification effectively, we should employ positive terms such as the *rest of faith, full salvation,* and *salvation to the uttermost.*

If our message is confirmed by reason and experience and the Bible, then our preaching must be *theologically* sound and psychologically credible. Just as no passage of scripture is isolated from others, so no doctrine can be unrelated to other doctrines. Almost all the historical doctrines of the Atonement relate only to justification. Obviously theologians historically have missed something here. Our preaching of holiness and entire sanctification must be related to the work of Christ on the Cross. Thus the admonition earlier to "preach Christ."

We must clarify our message *psychologically.* We live in a psychologically oriented world. Things are different since Sigmund Freud. The preacher of holiness must not forget that God works within the limits of humanity. We must avoid leaving the impression that entire sanctification involves the "destruction of the self." Jesus taught us that the self, the real self, is the person. Rather than speaking of the "death *of* the self," we should talk about the "death *to* the self."

Psychology can help us understand better our motivations, differences, limitations, and desires. However, psychological theories come and go. Consequently, it is a grave error to tie our holiness preaching to an outmoded psychological theory. Psychology can assist us in illustrating biblical truth but must never become a substitute for it.

The preacher of holiness (holy living) must clarify the holiness message *ethically.* Guidelines based on Scripture must be delineated to equip the entirely sanctified for all of life's relationships. The New Testament, and the Old Testament as well, must be preached, and not current ideas that are merely socially and culturally conditioned. Normal spiritual growth, however, will include an ever enlarging social consciousness and a passion for justice and righteousness in the affairs of nations and people.

Christian Assurance (See Part II, pp. 134-35.)

One of the distinctives of the Wesleyan message of holiness is that one can know he or she has been totally cleansed from in-being sin. The preacher of holiness must be prepared to declare how one knows this work of grace has been accomplished.

Clearly we do not know by our feelings, which tend to fluctuate depending upon circumstances. Rather, we know by the *fruit* and *witness* of the Spirit. The distinctive Wesleyan doctrine of assurance rests upon these biblical elements. Christian assurance includes the *objective* witness of the Spirit, which is simply God's Word and promise (e.g., 1 John 1:9; Deut. 30:6).

But we know also by the *subjective* witness of the Spirit, which involves the *direct* witness—there is no condemnation but a sense of ease and acceptance in the presence of

God (Rom. 8:1). The *indirect* subjective witness is the fruit of the Spirit manifest in our lives by the power of the Spirit (Gal. 5:22-23). The Spirit of Christ modeled in the marketplace and rough-and-tumble of life verifies the work of God's grace in us and assures us of our favor with God.

Growth in Grace (See Part II, pp. 124-25, 141-42.)

The article of faith titled "Entire Sanctification" in the 1993-97 *Manual of the Church of the Nazarene* includes the following two enlightening paragraphs:

> We believe that there is a marked distinction between a *pure* [perfect] heart and a *mature* [perfect] character. The former is obtained in an instant, the result of entire sanctification; the latter is the result of growth in grace.
>
> We believe that the grace of entire sanctification includes the impulse to grow in grace. However, this impulse must be consciously nurtured, and careful attention given to the requisites and processes of spiritual development and improvement in Christlikeness of character and personality. Without such purposeful endeavor one's witness may be impaired and the grace itself frustrated and ultimately lost.[8]

This progressive life is seen in 2 Cor. 3:18 (NKJV): "But we all, with unveiled face, beholding as in a mirror the glory of the Lord, are being transformed into the same image from glory to glory, just as by the Spirit of the Lord."

Those who have imagined that entire sanctification is the end of spiritual development have not begun to grasp the height and depth and breadth of the meaning of holiness. This experience or relationship with God through Christ opens up unimaginable possibilities of grace while eliminating the primary hindrance to growth, namely, the spirit of self-sovereignty.

Because there has been a death to the sinful self, the entirely sanctified is enabled to acknowledge failure and becomes increasingly dependent upon Christ. The entirely sanctified believer makes every effort to restore broken relationships. Such a Christian is not slow to make apology where another has been inadvertently or unknowingly injured. In fact, one's spiritual maturity may be measured by the length of time one allows to elapse between one's consciousness of failure, or the moment the Spirit reproves one, and one's efforts toward reconciliation.

The task of the preacher of holiness is to assist the believer to "walk worthy of the calling" (Eph. 4:1, NKJV). Paul always put side by side doctrine and duty, dogma and discipline, creed and conduct. Christian holiness is nothing if it does not alter our ethics. I once heard Ralph Bell of the Billy Graham Evangelistic Association say: "It is not enough to talk; the Christian must walk his faith daily." The believer's course of life must be distinctive. Our goal is to "present every man perfect in Christ Jesus" (Col. 1:28).

God will honor the preaching of holiness and will reward those who diligently seek Him. Paul makes this abundantly clear: "And the very God of peace sanctify you wholly; and I pray God your whole spirit and soul and body be preserved blameless unto the coming of our Lord Jesus Christ. *Faithful is he that calleth you, who also will do it"* (1 Thess. 5:23-24).

II

IN HIS LIKENESS:

God's Plan for a Holy People

"Ye know that the great end of religion is, to renew our hearts in the image of God, to repair that total loss of righteousness and true holiness which we sustained by the sin of our first parents. Ye know that all religion which does not answer to this end, all that stops short of this, the renewal of our soul in the *image of God*, after the *likeness of Him* that created it, is no other than a poor farce, and a mere mockery of God, to the destruction of our own soul" (italics mine).

—John Wesley (*Standard Sermons* 2:225)

| 3 |

Holiness:
The Possibility of Godlikeness

"The essence of true holiness consists in conformity to the nature and will of God"
(Samuel Lucas).

Knowing what God requires and how the divine requirements can be met should capture the attention of every thinking person. The Scriptures leave no doubt as to what God expects of man. Both Old and New Testaments reveal His demand: "Be ye holy, for I am holy" (Lev. 19:2; 1 Pet. 1:16).

This divine standard, however, is neither arbitrary nor capricious. God offers what He requires. His love precedes His law. The entire record of redemption is the story of God's efforts to enable man to become what he was created to be. His desire is to establish "a holy people," free from all sin, and to reproduce the divine image in man.

In the light of God's injunction to holiness and the means provided to fulfill the divine requirement, the widespread confusion concerning this fundamental teaching is difficult to understand. Too often human opinion and speculation have supplanted the plain declarations of God's Word. While there is room for varying interpretations on secondary points, the path to holiness is sufficiently clear so that no penitent seeker after truth should miss the way (Isa. 35:8).

God has placed before the mind and heart of man His own holiness as an incentive to purity and holy living. He makes His own perfection the standard of man's relative completeness and rectitude. Thus Jesus, the fullest Revelation of God, declared: "Be ye therefore perfect, even as your Father which is in heaven is perfect" (Matt. 5:48).

The obvious place to begin in seeking to discover what holiness means for man is to reflect on the holiness of God as set forth in the Scriptures. We should be reminded, however, that abstract thinking is not the pattern of the biblical writers. They thought in concrete terms of everyday living and came to know the living God as He revealed himself personally in the events of their lives and history.

To discuss the holiness of God, then, is not to consider some aspect of the existence of a God who is far removed from man. It is to discuss what God is like by looking at the active ways through which He relates himself to man, and (as we will do particularly in chapter 6) by turning our eyes upon the death and resurrection of Jesus, the living embodiment of God's likeness.

In so doing, we should be able to see God's plan for His people—what He wants us to be and do, for His holiness is the *pattern* as well as the *possibility* and *power* of being godlike.

THE HOLINESS OF GOD

The highest acknowledgment man can make of God is to say that He is "holy." Holiness is the foundation on which the whole conception of God rests. It is the background and atmosphere out of which an understanding of the divine activity develops. All salvation doctrines have their base in the holiness of God.

An adequate understanding of man's holiness presupposes the being of a God who is holy and whose design is the impartation of His holiness to man. No greater gift can be granted to man than the offer of sharing the divine life—God's holy nature.

Yet, however decisive for human life, however much we may comprehend it, we can never describe fully this quality of the character of God. This is because God's holiness is not just one among many of the divine attributes. It is so inherently a quality of God as to belong to the very nature of Divinity. To deny God's holiness is to deny the sacred reality that constitutes Deity.

The chief Hebrew word for "holiness" is *qodesh*, which, with its cognates, appears more than 830 times in the Old Testament. It is the most intimate word of all words used in reference to God. The word has "to do with those things and affairs in which God and man are involved together, that borderland where the human and the supra-human may be said to overlap."[1] Therefore, we must approach our study of God's holiness with a spirit of deep reverence and awe.

A. God's Holiness Is Unique

A good clue to one meaning of the word *holy*, as it relates to God, is its liturgical use. One of the first hymns to be found in most hymnals is "Holy, Holy, Holy, Lord God Almighty." The third stanza reads: *"Only* Thou art holy—there is none beside Thee / Perfect in pow'r, in love, in purity."

This aspect of God's holiness, His uniqueness, is expressed in various scriptures: "Who is like unto thee, O LORD, . . . glorious in holiness . . . ?" (Exod. 15:11); "To whom then will ye liken me, or shall I be equal? saith the

Holy One" (Isa. 40:25); "Who shall not fear thee, O Lord, and glorify thy name? for thou only art holy" (Rev. 15:4). The biblical statement that "no man" may look on God "and live" (Exod. 33:20) expresses the fear that the divine holiness inspires.

1. *Holiness and the Transcendence of God*

These verses declare the majesty, the glory, the sovereignty, the unfathomable mystery that mark only the Divine. God alone is said to be holy. No holiness exists except that which resides in God's own character or that which is imparted by Him to creatures.

God's holiness refers to His "otherness," to the distinction between the Creator and the creature. Hosea expressed this in the words of the Lord: "For I am God, and not man; the Holy One in the midst of thee" (11:9). The Hebrew word for "holy" *(qadosh)* has the root meaning of *that which is separate*. While holiness stands for the difference between God and man, it refers positively to what is God's, not negatively to what is not man's.

"God is separate and distinct because He is God. He is not separated *from* this, that, or the other because of any of His attributes or qualities or the like. A person or thing may be separate, or may come to be separated, because he or it has come to belong to God."[2]

2. *Holiness and the Service of God*

For this reason, holiness is ascribed to persons or things only in a derivative sense. When the Bible refers to holy places, holy men, holy angels, etc., it means that these are separated, "holy unto the Lord." That is, they belong to God; they are channels of His relation to men.

The word *separated*, when used to convey the meaning of holiness, denotes "separated to" as well as "separated from." Separation is not an end in itself. It is always for a positive and distinct purpose.

This truth has significant implications for man's holiness. The separation included in the holiness (or sanctifying) of things or men is not mere withdrawal *from* something. When applied to things, "holiness" does not mean separation in the sense of "lying apart." It always signifies "separated for deity, or belonging to the sphere of deity."[3]

When "holiness" is ascribed to God's people, it implies separation from that which is common, the world, *for the purpose of appropriation by God*. It is separation for a higher goal, for service to man.

B. God's Holiness Is Pure

The prophets and New Testament writers emphasized the personal and moral character of God's holiness. Isaiah declared: "For thus saith the high and lofty One that inhabiteth eternity, whose name is Holy; I dwell in the high and holy place, with him also that is of a contrite and humble spirit, to revive the spirit of the humble, and to revive the heart of the contrite ones" (57:15).

Habakkuk asserted God's holiness or moral purity, His repugnance of the unclean in man (though he wondered at God's delay of judgment): "Thou art of purer eyes than to behold evil, and canst not look on iniquity" (1:13). The psalmist spoke strongly of the moral quality of God's holiness: "Thou lovest righteousness, and hatest wickedness" (45:7).

God is *absolutely* holy because He possesses in His own nature all possible moral goodness to the exclusion of every kind and degree of moral evil. Holiness in God is that upright constitution of His being that causes Him to abhor sin and admire purity. It prompts Him to retard all moral evil, consistent with man's freedom and responsibility. The complete moral separation of God stands in contrast to all that is unholy and profane, to all that is contrary to His upright nature.

1. *Separateness from Sin*

The primary meaning of the scriptural teaching of holiness as it relates to God is His separateness *from sin*. No sin can be admitted into His immediate presence. When the psalmist asked, "Who shall stand in his holy place?" the reply given was "he that hath clean hands, and a pure heart; who hath not lifted up his soul unto vanity, nor sworn deceitfully" (24:3-4).

Jesus and the writer of Hebrews express the same truth: "Blessed are the pure in heart: for they shall see [enjoy] God" (Matt. 5:8); "Follow peace with all men, and holiness, without which no man shall see the Lord" (Heb. 12:14).

Not only is God *separated* from sin, but also He is eternally *opposed* to sin. It is the very opposite of His nature. Being holy, He seeks the banishment of sin from His universe. God's judgment upon sin because of His holy nature is seen throughout the Scriptures. Nowhere is it more clearly revealed than at Calvary, where a holy God brings judgment upon sin. "A holy God, separate from sin, could not spare His own Son when that Son, who knew no sin, was made sin for us and suffered the punishment for our sins, the sins of the world."[4]

Because God's holiness designates His purity in contrast and opposition to everything that is corrupt or unclean, it goes beyond His majesty to include His moral perfection. "Immaculate sanctity is so involved in the Christian idea of God, that if the attribute of purity could be separated from His character, the conception of supreme Deity would be banished from the mind."[5]

2. *Man's Uncleanness*

The classic biblical passage in which the holiness of God is portrayed as purity is Isaiah 6. God's spokesman to Judah here mourned the death of King Uzziah in the Temple. Prostrate before the Lord, he was given a glimpse of the holiness of God: "I saw also the Lord sitting upon a throne, high and lifted up, and his train filled the temple. . . . the seraphims . . . cried unto [one] another, and said, Holy, holy, holy, is the LORD of hosts: the whole earth is full of his glory. And the posts of the door moved at the voice of him that cried, and the house was filled with smoke."

A vivid conception of the divine purity awakened a penitential realization of personal uncleanness in the great prophet, who confessed: "Woe is me! for I am undone; because I am a man of unclean lips, and I dwell in the midst of a people of unclean lips: for mine eyes have seen the King, the LORD of hosts."

As shadows are deep in proportion to the brilliance of the sun, so the depravity of the human heart is more distinctly outlined by comparison with the holiness of God. Isaiah's terror before God's majesty evoked deep acknowledgment and confession of sin, resulting in divine cleansing. One of the seraphim took a live coal from off the altar, laid it on the prophet's mouth, and said: "Lo, this hath touched thy lips; and thine iniquity is taken away, and thy sin purged."

Isaiah noted also that God's "train filled the temple," stressing His immanence. He is not only "high and lifted up" but also near and accessible. Because God is transcendent and pure, holiness is demanded; because He is immanent and gracious, holiness is possible.

3. *The Glory of God*

The dramatic experience of Isaiah illustrates a further concept associated with God's holiness. Holiness as it relates to the Divine Presence encompasses the idea of *brilliance*. Here the affinity with the concept of "glory" is seen. Numerous passages speak of holiness that is linked with God's presence and radiance, such as the burning bush, described as "holy ground" (Exod. 3:5). His presence in the Tabernacle or the Temple was manifested by a fiery radiance filling the place of worship (Exod. 40:34-38; 2 Chron. 7:1 ff.).

The pillar of fire was an indication to Israel of God's presence (Exod. 14:24). The Book of Ezekiel oft uses the word "holiness" in representing the divine glory as a "bright and fiery presence" (10:4). At the dedication of Solomon's Temple "the cloud filled the house of the LORD, so that the priests could not stand to minister because of the cloud: for the glory of the LORD had filled the house of the LORD" (1 Kings 8:10-11). Later Jewish tradition spoke of this experience, and of the manifest presence of the Lord, as His "*Shekinah*," or glory.

God wills "that the whole earth be filled with his glory" (Ps. 72:19), that men should know and confess His name (Phil. 2:10-11). His holy name and His glory are inseparable. The revelation of the holy God has attained its end where the "glory of the Lord" is "mirrored" (see NKJV) in the hearts of believers (2 Cor. 3:18). There is then a moral quality in the idea of God's glory, for in the holy presence of God one is made aware of his own uncleanness and unworthiness, his inability to radiate or reflect the divine glory.

C. God's Holiness Is Righteous

The eighth-century prophets—Amos, Hosea, Isaiah, and Micah—gave a further dimension to the meaning of God's holiness. The actual words "holiness" and "holy" are not often used in their writings, with the exception of Isaiah. However, each of them reiterated the fact that God by His very nature (that is, because of His holiness) demands right conduct from His worshipers and will be content with nothing less.

1. *The Ethical Character of Holiness*

Isaiah clearly and specifically connected holiness and righteousness: "But the LORD of hosts shall be exalted in judgment, and God that is holy shall be sanctified in righteousness" (5:16). The term "exalted" is an equivalent of the Hebrew word meaning "be sanctified." Therefore the prophet was saying that this sanctifying or hallowing of the holy God is to be done in "righteousness." That is, men will see the holiness of God by the exaltation or demonstration of righteous conduct in their midst.

In his own way each of these prophets associated holiness and righteousness. Amos condemned those who oppressed the poor and who failed to see that bribery and corruption with its perversion of ordinary justice between man and man is a negation of one's religious practice and testimony. In the light of God's command to "hate the evil, and love the good," Amos fervently prayed: "Let judgment run down as waters, and righteousness as a mighty stream" (5:24; cf. 2:6-8; 5:7-10, 21-23).

Hosea complained that there was no trustworthiness anywhere, "no truth, nor mercy [loyalty], nor knowledge of God in the land" (4:1). He expressed God's standard of social conduct: "I desired mercy, and not sacrifice; and the knowledge of God more than burnt offerings" (6:6). Because of the people's sin God would not accept their sacrifices (8:11, 13).

Isaiah observed that the people honored God with their lips, but not in their hearts. They called evil good, and good evil. Where the prophet looked for judgment, he found oppression; and instead of righteousness, he heard a cry. Everywhere men were profane evildoers, practicing drunkenness, bribery, and corruption (1:23; 5:7, 11-12, 20, 22; 29:13).

Like Amos, Micah charged the rich with oppression of the poor and spoke against those who lie awake at night to think out new schemes whereby they can rob the poor man of what little he has. Even priests and prophets were out for all they could get, thinking of nothing save accumulating wealth. Micah gave a good summary of the preaching of these classical prophets in his famous passage: "Wherewith shall I come before the LORD, and bow myself before the high God? shall I come before him with burnt offerings . . . ? He hath shewed thee, O man, what is good; and what doth the LORD require of thee, but to do justly, and to love mercy, and to walk humbly with thy God?" (6:6-8; cf. 2:1-2; 3:11).

The point is that these prophets had an understanding of righteousness that grew out of their knowledge of God and His holiness. They did not judge human conduct merely by an ethical code. Their standard was what they knew of the nature of God himself.

2. *Justice and Love*

Being righteous and just, God requires the same virtues in man. If His holiness involves righteousness, then man cannot be accepted of God while living in sin or tolerating injustice. To live as though religion is one thing and "business" or "politics" another, two worlds that can never meet, is an affront to a holy God and will incur His judgment.

The "Holiness Code" (Lev. 17—26) shows the same indissoluble connection between worship and work, religious devotion and ethical practice, by combining ritual law and moral law. The injunctions within it, such as "Thou shalt love thy neighbour as thyself: I am the LORD" (19:18), make clear that the only holiness acceptable to God is that which involves right and just relations with all men.

This strong ethical emphasis is continued in the New Testament, which also equates holiness or moral purity with righteous conduct. The language is explicit: "Put on therefore, as the elect of God, holy and beloved, bowels of mercies, kindness, humbleness of mind, meekness, longsuffering" (Col. 3:12); "For as ye have yielded your members servants to uncleanness and to iniquity unto iniquity; even so now yield your members servants to *righteousness unto holiness*" (Rom. 6:19); "*That no man go beyond and defraud his brother* in any matter: . . . *For God hath not called us* unto uncleanness, *but unto holiness*" (1 Thess. 4:6-7); "Dearly beloved, let us cleanse ourselves from all filthiness of the flesh and spirit, *perfecting holiness in the fear of God*" (2 Cor. 7:1); "And the Lord make you to *increase and abound in love one toward another, and toward all men* . . . To the end he may stablish your hearts *unblameable in holiness before God*, even our Father, at the coming of our Lord Jesus Christ" (1 Thess. 3:12-13).

GOD'S HOLINESS AND MAN'S

The holiness of God refers to two basic truths with regard to His being: (1) *He is separate, unique, distinctive.* His holiness has to do with His transcendence or "otherness" (not to be confused with remoteness or "awayness"). Thus man stands before Him in awe and reverence. (2) *He is pure, upright, and righteous.* This aspect of His holiness expresses His immanence or nearness, for He desires to share His purity with man. Thus man should bow before Him in confession and penitence.

R. F. Weidmer asserts: "Two things lie in the divine holiness. 1) God stands apart and in opposition to the world, and 2) He removes this opposition by a redemptive offer of communion with Himself."[6] God wills that man should be filled with His glory and should have a share in that quality that is His alone. "Thus the holiness of God is the basis of the self-communication which is fulfilled in love."[7] The Holy One is the Redeemer or Savior!

Though God in His holiness is separate and "wholly other," He yet longs to enter into a personal and intimate relationship with man and to share with man His glory and purity. Concerning this paradox H. Orton Wiley wrote that "the love of God is in fact the desire to impart holiness, and this desire is satisfied only when the beings whom it seeks are rendered holy."[8]

This benevolent intention existed in God in eternity, prior to the beginning of time (Eph. 1:4). God both creates the desire in man for His holiness and provides the means for its fulfillment. Indeed, all His dealings with His children are intended to produce holiness in them—to create a holy people. He even chastens us "for our profit, that we might be partakers of his holiness" (Heb. 12:10).

Two fundamental themes of the Scriptures, running through both Old and New Testaments, bear witness to the overwhelming truth that God desires to share with men His holiness, His nature, His purity. These themes are: the idea of the covenant; and man in the image of God.

A. God's Gracious Covenant

The doctrine of election, a leading biblical concept, is based upon the holiness of God. The "holy" are the "elect" (1 Pet. 1:2). The "elect," "his own," are all those who "receive him" in His revelation, who respond to the offer and condition of His covenant (John 1:12).

The covenant of Sinai established Israel as a national unit, and thereafter Hebrew religion was the religion of God's chosen people. United Israel became a "holy people." To Israel, God said: "Now therefore, if you will obey my voice and keep my covenant, you shall be *my own possession* among all peoples, for all the earth is mine, and you shall be to me a kingdom of priests and *an holy* nation" (Exod. 19:5-6, RSV).

1. *The Demand for Obedience*

God himself was the Originator of the covenant. He

alone stated its terms and drew up the precepts that Israel must obey if the covenant were to continue. By the covenant, Israel was admitted to God's sphere of life, and thus she was *sanctified*. By admitting Israel, God by no means gave up His own holiness, but Israel was sanctified in her *communion* with Him.[9] Israel's holiness thus was a gift conditioned upon her continual obedience.

The fact that God laid down the conditions under which the covenant would endure is indicative of His holiness and righteousness, which provides the *absolute* standard of right and wrong. Whatever is in accord with His holiness is right; what is not in accord with His holiness is wrong. The requirements of the moral law with their consequent penalties pronounced upon those breaking that law are manifestations of the holiness of God (see, e.g., Ezek. 18:4).

2. *A Holy People*

God, who is holy, wants and seeks a people who are holy. For this reason He chose Israel and has constituted the Church, the new Israel, to be *separate, dedicated, consecrated*, or *set apart* to a particular function for His glory.

In this idea of a holy people we see one of the fundamental meanings of the word *holy*. It means, as suggested earlier, to be *"consecrated to God's service."* This concept of holiness, commonly referred to as "ceremonial holiness," sometimes in the Scriptures is applied to times, to things, and even to persons (e.g., Exod. 3:5—"holy ground"; 35:2—"holy days"; Lev. 27:30—"holy tithe"; 2 Chron. 35:13—"holy offerings"; Acts 3:21—"holy prophets"; Eph. 3:5—"holy apostles and prophets"). In such cases the adjective "holy" means "possession by God," or "dedication to God," and implies no moral quality as such, although some ethical content is related to it.

The verb *"sanctify"* means "to make holy" and is applied to both things and persons (e.g., Exod. 29:36—"altar"; Deut. 5:12—"Sabbath"; Exod. 19:22—"priests"; Matt. 23:19—"altar . . . sanctifieth the gift"; 1 Cor. 7:14—believing spouse "sanctifies the unbelieving" mate; John 10:36—"the Father hath sanctified . . . the Son"; 17:19—Christ sanctified himself). The word *"sanctify"* in this sense is virtually equivalent to the words *consecrate* or *set apart*. Occasionally, signifying this restricted meaning, it is stated that men are to do the sanctifying (1 Pet. 3:15).

God's desire for, and promise of, a holy people is seen in the New Testament to be fulfilled in the Christian Church:

> But you are a chosen race, a royal priesthood, a holy nation, God's own people [literally, "a people for his possession"], that you may declare the *wonderful deeds of him* who called you out of darkness into his marvelous light. Once you were no people but now you are God's people; once you had not received mercy but now you have received mercy *(1 Pet. 2:9-10, RSV).*

3. *God's Called-out Ones*

As "holy" in the Old Testament is used both of God and of the people whom the Lord called out from among the nations, so, in the New Testament, the words associated with "holy" describe the Church, which has been called out of the world. The term *hagiois* (literally, "holy ones") is translated "saints" in the King James or Authorized Version. Paul habitually addressed the New Testament believers as "saints" (Rom. 1:7; Eph. 4:12).

Consistent with the Old Testament emphasis on holiness as *separation,* all members of the Church, those who have been baptized into Christ, are "sanctified in Christ Jesus" (1 Cor. 1:2). We may infer, as Reformation theology does, that all Christians are "sanctified" by virtue of being in Christ in the sense of being separated from the world and devoted to God.

George Allen Turner points out that "this means the ascription of *sanctity* [holiness] to persons or (things) by virtue of a *relationship* to Deity, a relationship resulting from separation from the common and unclean, and dedication to God."[10] This has been called "positional sanctification."

4. *The New Covenant*

To this point the meanings of "holiness" and "sanctification" are essentially synonymous in both Testaments. However, the New Testament brings to fruition a seed idea from the Old that was only partially and slowly perceived by the ancient writers.

The author of Deuteronomy made clear that God desires a holy people, a "people of inheritance" (4:20; 7:6-8; 9:29). The idea of a holy people was developed by the prophets, who combined with it the concept of the "righteous remnant" as a holy community (Isa. 10:20-22; Jer. 23:3; 31:7; Amos 5:15; Mic. 1:7). Jeremiah went further and promised a *new covenant*, which can apply only to the holy remnant and would be fulfilled with the coming of Christ:

> Behold, the days come, saith the LORD, that I will make a new covenant with the house of Israel, and with the house of Judah: not according to the covenant that I made with their fathers in the day that I took them by the hand to bring them out of the land of Egypt; . . . but this shall be the covenant that I will make with the house of Israel; After those days, saith the LORD, *I will put* my law in their inward parts, and write it in their hearts; and will be their God, and they shall be my people *(31:31-33).*

Under the new covenant God would deal with the mainsprings of human action. Religion would no longer be merely external; inwardness would be the dominant note. Heretofore the laws of God had been written on tables of stone; under the new covenant they would be written in the heart, so that men would respond to God from inward motivation.[11]

With a different figure of speech Ezekiel echoed the same promise of the Lord:

> Then will I sprinkle clean water upon you, and *ye shall be clean:* from all your filthiness, and from all your idols, will I cleanse you. *A new heart also will I give you,* and a *new spirit* will I put *within* you: and I will take away the stony heart out of your flesh, and I will give you an heart of flesh. And I will put my spirit within you, and *cause you to walk in my statutes,* and ye shall keep my judgments, and do them *(36:25-27).*

5. *Personal and Inward Holiness*

In fulfillment of these prophecies the *primary* meaning of holiness in the New Testament is *internalized,* evidenced outwardly by righteous conduct. The Temple regarded as holy is the *"household* of God, with all the saints, Jesus Christ himself being the chief corner stone" (Eph. 2:19-20). The "holy sacrifice" demanded is the *living sacrifice* of the believer's body (Rom. 12:1). Moral purification or *ethical sanctification of the heart* from sin (Acts 15:8-9) becomes central under the new covenant and encompasses an internal renovation of the self (John 17).

By a new covenant God separates a people to himself through the redemption that is in Christ Jesus (1 Cor. 1:30-31). Therefore, the author of Hebrews quotes Jeremiah's prophecy, "I will put my laws into their hearts, and in their minds will I write them." Then he adds:

> And their sins and iniquities will I remember no more. . . . Having, therefore, brethren, boldness to enter into the holiest by the blood of Jesus, by a new and

living way, which he hath consecrated for us through the veil, that is to say, his flesh; and having an high priest over the house of God; let us draw near with a true heart in full assurance of faith, having our hearts sprinkled from an evil conscience, and our bodies washed with pure water" (10:17, 19-22).

Thus to the Son He sware, and said
With Thee My covenant first is made;
In Thee shall dying sinners live,
Glory and grace are Thine to give.

My covenant I will ne'er revoke,
But keep My grace in mind;
And what eternal love hath spoke,
Eternal truth shall bind.
                                    —ISAAC WATTS

B. Man in the Image of God

The outstanding feature of the conception of man in the Old Testament is the pronouncement that man was created in God's image, after His likeness (Gen. 1:26 ff.; 5:1; 9:6b; Ps. 8:5). While the Father-son image was only seldom used by Old Testament writers to denote the relation between God and His people, yet the expressions "the image of God" and "likeness of God" (which essentially mean the same) were intended to depict the intimate relationship as between father and child, as implied in Gen. 5:3, where Adam's son is said to be in the "likeness" and "image" of his father.

1. *The Sons of God*

Throughout the New Testament, God's relationship to those who do His will is expressed by the figure of Father and son:

As many as received him, to them gave he power to become the *sons of God*, even to them that believe on his name *(John 1:12)*; Wherefore thou *art no more a servant, but a son;* and if a son, then an heir of God through Christ *(Gal. 4:7)*; Behold, what manner of love the Father hath bestowed upon us, that we should be *called the sons of God (1 John 3:1)*; Do all things without murmurings and disputings: that ye may be blameless and harmless, *the sons of God,* without rebuke, in the midst of a crooked and perverse nation, among whom ye shine as lights in the world *(Phil. 2:14-15)*.

2. *Conformed to Christ's Image*

By virtue both of being created in God's likeness and of becoming His sons by redemption, man is to be like God. In the beginning God was so appreciative of holiness and moral purity that He resolved to make man initially after this glorious prototype. Thus man was created holy with a capacity to bear the divine image. Though man fell into sin and forfeited the moral and spiritual aspect of this likeness, God's original purpose remains unchanged. Therefore He sent His Son, "Christ, who is the *image* of God" (2 Cor. 4:4), to restore the primary, but now lost, rectitude of human nature.

The original prototype—the image of God, fully known in Jesus—is both the divine standard and glorious *possibility* for man. Of this great truth we are assured and admonished by Paul: "And that ye put on the new man, which after God is *created in righteousness and true holiness*" (Eph. 4:24). The "new man" is the moral character of God, the spirituality of His nature, as revealed in Jesus Christ.

In Christ we have "given unto us exceeding great and precious promises: that by these ye might be *partakers of the divine nature*, having escaped the corruption that is in the world through lust" (2 Pet. 1:4). In Him we have been chosen "to be conformed to the *image* of . . . [God's] Son" (Rom. 8:29).

To be in the image of God, to share His holiness, is to

be transformed into the *image of Christ,* for in Christ "dwelt all the fulness [including holiness] of the Godhead bodily" (Col. 2:9). For this reason we are exhorted: "Let this mind be in you, which was also in Christ Jesus" (Phil. 2:5).

The basic and felt need of every man, whether or not he is aware of it, is to be "in the image of God." David eloquently expressed this universal longing: "As for me, I will behold thy face in righteousness: I shall be *satisfied,* when I *awake with thy likeness*" (Ps. 17:15). Where the likeness of God is not reimpressed upon the soul, there is no enduring satisfaction. Where it is present, there is an inner sense of fulfillment, peace of heart, and "rest" of faith (Heb. 4:9).

CONCLUSION

These fundamental ideas of Scripture—the covenant and the image of God—embody two great truths, which at first may appear to be mutually exclusive, but which together elucidate a balanced view of the holiness of God. On the one hand, God, by initiating the covenant, has called to himself "a holy people." As He is unique and distinct from man in His holiness, so also He requires His people to be set apart, separated for His purposes.

On the other hand, by creating man in His own image and offering the possibility of recreating him in Jesus Christ, He actually *shares* His holiness with men. As He is pure and righteous, so God expects men to be spiritually clean and morally upright. The divine holiness involves the positive activity of that Personal Other, who continuously seeks to make men in His likeness.

> *Eternal Spirit, write Thy law*
> *Upon our inward parts,*
> *And let the Second Adam draw*
> *His image on our hearts.*
> —ISAAC WATTS

4

Sin:
The Loss of Godlikeness

"Holiness in us is the copy or transcript of the holiness that is in Christ" (Philip Henry).

Because God's love impels Him to share His holiness, His nature, He created "man in his own image" (Gen. 1:27). That man's highest destiny is to bear the moral image of God is indicated either explicitly or implicitly throughout the Bible (e.g., Eph. 4:24; Col. 3:10).

The terms "image" and "likeness" are used interchangeably in the Scriptures to denote man's kinship to Deity (cf. Gen. 1:26-27; 5:1, 3). Since "God is a Spirit" (John 4:24) without body or physical parts,[1] the image referred to must be spiritual. To be made in His likeness is to be given a moral character like that of God, or godlikeness.

SOMETHING HAS HAPPENED

God's holiness could not permit Him to create a man as anything but good (Gen. 1:31), "perfect" (Ezek. 28:12, 15), and "upright" (Eccles. 7:29). But any cursory view of history or contemporary life will show that man is different from the way the Bible declares he was created. Something is drastically wrong with man, with the human race. Christian faith identifies this "wrongness" as "sin," the denial of holiness and opposition to the nature and character of God.

The biblical record affirms that sin is an intruder. It is not "original" in the sense of being a part of the primordial makeup of man. It is a monstrous perversion and defilement of God's good creation. To say otherwise would make God himself responsible and would contradict everything we know about His holiness. Sin is an alien element, antagonistic to God and the noblest interests of men. It is not "subject to the law of God, neither indeed can be" (Rom. 8:7).

BUT THERE'S GOOD NEWS!

The "good news" is that God through Christ has made possible a complete deliverance from sin and a perfect reproduction of His image of righteousness and true holiness in this life. To appreciate and appropriate this grand provision, we must understand the meaning and nature of sin. Otherwise there is danger of minimizing or misunderstanding the person and work of Christ.

For this reason J. B. Chapman observed that "men's conception of sin is fundamental to all their thinking and speaking on soteriology."[2] The doctrine of sin is the center around which one's entire theological system is formed.

Therefore in this chapter and the next we will consider various aspects of sin in order to comprehend more fully our "so great salvation" (Heb. 2:3). Here we will discuss man's fall into sin, the origin of sin, sin as disobedience and defiance, loss of the image of God, and Adam's sin and original sin.

MAN'S FALL INTO SIN

When the Bible speaks of sin, it does not normally remind us of the account of the Fall, though it is everywhere assumed. Apart from acceptance of the fall of man, it is impossible to understand sin as the presupposition of the New Testament message of redemption.

Only a *fallen* humanity needs a Redeemer. Every conception of sin that is not established upon this teaching either denies sin's existence or minimizes its seriousness by making it a fact of nature or merely a moral concern of the individual. The latter alternative must assert that man, given sufficient time and favorable conditions, by his own efforts can overcome sin or eliminate it—a claim disproven by all of history.

The nature of sin has been viewed in many ways. It has been said that what is called "sin" is ignorance; that it is a mere illusion; that it is a false subordination of reason to sense; that it is a carryover of animal qualities from lower stages of existence; that it is a necessary limitation of finite being; that it is a social or economic imbalance that will be corrected through some dialectical process of nature; that it grows out of an eternal principle of evil; or that it is material and is directly related to man's sensuous nature. All such philosophical humanistic theories fail to see the intractable power and *personal* character of sin involving a broken relationship with a holy God.

THE ORIGIN OF SIN

Many attempts to explain the origin of sin have been made. None are satisfactory. Nor could they be, for if the "cause" of sin could be identified, then responsibility for it would be removed from man to some prior source. But the essence of sin is man's refusal to accept responsibility, which always leads him to blame someone or something other than himself (Gen. 3:11-13).

Suffice it to say that sin is a consequence of the abuse and misuse of man's freedom. Beyond this, reason cannot go, and revelation is silent. Man was created with moral capability, with the power of self-determination or moral choice. This endowment carried with it the power to choose evil as well as good. All of God's moral creatures, both angels and men, were constituted with an option and ability to throw off God's restraints and go their own chosen way.

That is, God, who desires a free response to His overtures of holiness and love, made man in such a way that sin was a possibility. Sin therefore is *personal* in its origin. Whatever else remains unclear, it is certain that all the responsibility for the beginning and continuance of sin in man, and the practice of it by man, rests with man himself.

SIN AS DISOBEDIENCE AND DEFIANCE

God made known His supreme will to Adam and Eve, our foreparents. But under Satan's influence, yet freely and thus in a blameworthy act, they knowingly disobeyed a law that God had given them for their good (Gen. 3:1-6). Their sin was transgression of a law. Not just any law, or law in general, but the law of God. The essential and exclusive view of the Bible is stated by the psalmist: "Against thee, thee only, have I sinned" (51:4). Sin is not merely disregard for some ordinance, it is opposition to the living God! It is the self in rebellion against the sovereignty of God!

Thence, in the record of the Fall, sin is portrayed as *disobedience* to a personal, holy God, arising out of *distrust* and *defiance*. The fundamental motivation for this "original" or first sin was the desire to be "as God." Adam wanted to be on a level with God—to become self-directing and self-reliant. He refused to acknowledge that his godlikeness, his goodness, his holiness came by dependence on God. Therefore *pride* led him to turn away from God to self, insisting on his own "rights."

"The deepest root of sin is . . . the spiritual defiance of

the one who understands freedom as independence. Sin is emancipation from God, giving up the attitude of dependence, in order to try to win full independence, which makes man equal with God."[3] Though man is intended to be free and to be like God, he cannot have freedom and holiness apart from God. True freedom and holiness in man are derived gifts of God (John 8:31-36).

LOSS OF THE IMAGE OF GOD

This fall into sin disrupted man's communion with God, bringing fear and guilt instead of love (Gen. 3:7-10). No longer did he live "in the image of God." Man chose to make himself *in his own image,* a choice that deprived him of moral rectitude, of righteousness, of holiness, and of his ability to do right (cf. Job 11:7-11; Jer. 10:23; Rom. 7:15). H. Orton Wiley has summarized the effect of sin on our first parents:

> The immediate consequences of man's sin were *estrangement from God, enslavement to Satan, and the loss of divine grace.* . . . Man no longer possessed the glory of his moral likeness to God. . . . Deprived of the Holy Spirit as the organizing principle of his being, there could be no harmonious ordering of his faculties, and hence his powers became disordered. From this disordered state there followed as a consequence: . . . unregulated carnal craving; and moral inability or weakness in the presence of sin.[4]

Prior to the Fall, because of God's enabling grace and imparted holiness, Adam was "able not to sin." Following the Fall, he was *deprived* of the presence and power of God and therefore was "not able not to sin."

A. The Gift of Prevenient Grace

The fall of man, then, was from a "state of grace" to a "state of nature." He became a "natural" man. But God did not leave man in this predicament. Had all grace been withdrawn and withheld, man would have ceased to be a moral creature with responsibility. But this totally "natural" man does not exist, since the prevenient grace of God (the grace that "goes before") was given to sinful Adam and is given to every actual man in history, conferring upon him a degree of freedom and responsibility, and even enabling him to perform occasional acts of goodness.[5]

Prevenient grace restores sufficient moral freedom to enable man to reject or accept light, whether the light of the gospel or of nature, and to refrain from those sins or crimes that would destroy the social order. When we speak of the *total depravity* of man as a result of the Fall, we mean "total" in the sense that sin has pervaded and perverted *all* aspects of man's life. If sin were colored blue, every part of man would be some shade of blue.

Man's corruption, however, is not "total" in the sense that he cannot progress in wickedness, nor in the sense that his will has no ability to respond to God. Total depravity means that man is totally unable of himself to overcome sin. Yet God's prevenient grace restores a measure of freedom, enabling him either to accept or reject salvation.

B. The "Essential" Image and the "Spiritual" Image

Because of this grace given to man following the Fall—that "Light, which lighteth every man that cometh into the world" (John 1:9)—theologians have distinguished between the "essential," "natural," or "formal" image of God in man; and the "spiritual," "moral," or "material" image. The "essential" image is what makes man to be man, even in his sin. It refers to the elements of personality or selfhood: intellect, conscience, power of choice, immortality, the capacity to respond to God, and so on. These are *indelible* gifts of God. The "spiritual" image has to do with man's holiness, his godlikeness.

In our discussion of the "image of God" it must be clear that we are not referring to a *thing* or substance *in* man. Rather, the term is used to describe a relationship between man and God.

Man was not made with a choice as to *whether* he would respond to God. The fact *that* man must respond, *that* he is responsible, is fixed. No amount of human freedom, nor of the sinful misuse of freedom, can alter this fact. Responsibility is part of the unchangeable structure of man's being. This aspect of human nature, that which constitutes man's humanness in distinction from all other creatures, is part of the meaning of being created in God's image.

This "essential" or "natural" image cannot be lost so long as man is man. However, it has been impaired so that man's judgment is faulty and his body is subject to infirmity and death. It will not be restored totally until the next life, when man will be given a glorified body patterned after the resurrected body of Christ.

The other element of the image of God—the "spiritual" or "moral" image—has been *wholly* lost and not merely effaced. All of Scripture affirms that man failed to respond to God as his Maker intended, and thus he became alienated from the life of God—from His holiness and love. Man fashioned himself in his own image rather than in the spiritual image of God, which has been totally destroyed in the Fall.

To confuse these understandings of the image of God can lead to great error theologically. Without a proper distinction one might erroneously claim that loss of the image of God means the loss of the quality of humanity itself; or that man did not totally lose the image, it has only been impaired; or that so long as one remains a man, he cannot be restored to the image of God. None of these is acceptable. To hold to the first would be to say that the sinner is not really human, and thus not morally responsible. To accept the second or third is contrary to the teachings of the Scriptures.

ADAM'S SIN AND ORIGINAL SIN

In some inexplicable manner Adam's sin affected the entire human race. Experience shows that sin among men is universal, and the Bible notes an intrinsic relationship between the first man's sin and that of every man. Paul taught that "by one man sin entered into the world, and death by sin; and so death passed upon all men, for that all have sinned" (Rom. 5:12 ff.; see also 1 Cor. 15:45 ff.).

A. The Unity of the Race

No *explanation* of the transference of Adam's sin to succeeding generations is given in Scripture. Even Rom. 5:12, which on the surface may appear to provide an explanation, offers none. Paul was not trying to explain what the nature of sin is (at least this was not his primary purpose) or how it is transmitted. His point was to show that Christ has conquered death and brought life and salvation from sin.

To do this, the apostle referred to the Fall in order to say that "in Adam" all are sinners; "in Christ" all are redeemed. His intention was to expound the unity of the human race. He wanted to indicate that in Christ we see that humanity is one in sin, but that this unity of mankind is replaced by the unity of the redeemed. The reference to Adam, therefore, is not intended to *explain* the origin or presence of sin, nor to excuse man for his sinning. The reference to Adam's sin, and man's relationship to it, emphasizes the *universality* of sin, which is confirmed by both the Scriptures and experience.

Though Adam came under the curse of death, both physical and spiritual, and each human being comes under this ban, we do not know how sin is passed on. Various theories have been advanced to account for the transmission of sin to the entire human race,[6] all of which have limitations. John Wesley drew attention to the connection between Adam and the human race by referring to Adam as a "public person" and "the representative man."[7] Yet he refused to speculate regarding the *way* the race became involved in sin. He said:

> If you ask me, *how* . . . sin is propagated; *how* it is transmitted from father to son: I answer plainly, I cannot tell; no more than I can tell how a man is propagated, how a body is transmitted from father to son. I know both the one and the other fact; but I can account for neither.[8]

B. Deprivation and Depravity

Some theologians have suggested that man became *depraved* because he was *deprived* of that which was originally given to him. W. T. Purkiser, following this thought, has written:

> The answer to the puzzle may been seen in part when we reflect that in the Garden, by their first sin, Adam and Eve lost the holiness in which they were created, which was given to them by the presence of God. They became depraved because they were deprived of God's righteousness by their sin of disobedience and rebellion. They could not pass on what they did not possess; hence their race was depraved because deprived of the righteousness which its parents did not have. . . . Sin as a state or condition is more than the absence of righteousness; but it has its source in the loss of holiness just as blindness results from the loss of sight, and darkness from the absence of light.[9]

However it may be accounted for, the significant point is that in some real, though unknown, manner due to

Adam's transgression, "we are by nature children of wrath" (Eph. 2:3). Although the Authorized Version reads that "all have sinned" (Rom. 5:12), in light of the aorist tense employed in the Greek, a better translation would be "all sinned" (NIV). Thus in some sense we all sinned when Adam sinned.

For Paul, Adam is racially significant in the same way as is Christ. Therefore the apostle contrasted Adam with Christ in Rom. 5:12-21 and in 1 Cor. 15:21-22. As in Jesus Christ all have been redeemed, so in Adam all have sinned. Adam is not only the "first" man but also the "universal" man. The same universality, which in the one Christ includes all men, includes all men in the one Adam.

If being "in Christ" is to have His spirit of self-giving, humility, servitude, and obedience "unto death" (see Phil. 2), then being "in Adam" is to be under the control of his spirit of self-centeredness, self-exaltation, self-service, and self-assertion. Every man has his existence either "in Adam" or "in Christ."

C. Universal or Birth Sin

Throughout the history of Christian thought, the Church has proclaimed that Adam's sin has brought severe consequences to the human race. This racial corruption is summarized in Article VII, as abridged by Wesley, for the Methodist Church in America under the title "Of Original or Birth Sin":

Original sin standeth not in the following [of the example] of Adam (as the Pelagians do vainly talk), but it is the corruption of the nature of every man, that naturally is engendered of the offspring of Adam, whereby man is very far gone from original righteousness, and of his own nature inclined to evil, and that continually.

Much confusion has gathered around both the term itself and the meaning of this "birth" sin. Technically, the

term *original sin* should apply to "the" *original* sin, the first
sin, the personal act of Adam; and not to the racial consequences of Adam's sin, which should be described by the
term *inherited* or *universal* depravity.

Further, original sin, or man's sinful nature, should
not be confused or equated with the body, specifically with
sexuality, or concupiscence, as Augustine was inclined to
do. Original sin is not a biological fact, but a spiritual fact.
Sin does not have to do with chromosomes and genes, but
with the spiritual truth that sin is not something acciden-
tal. Sin is not "some-thing" in man, but the separation of
man's true existence from God and his resistance to God.

Being estranged from God, man loves darkness rather
than the light of God's holiness (John 3:19). This lost communion with God cannot be regained apart from a reconciling act of God himself. Original sin, an implacable rebellion against God, is inseparable from every man until
Christ breaks the bonds and sets him free.

The New Testament proclaims what God has done in
order to restore man's lost estate and break the power of
sin. It declares that Jesus, "who knew no sin" (2 Cor. 5:21),
is the true "image of God" (2 Cor. 4:4; Col. 1:15) that man
regains through faith "in Jesus Christ."

While the Bible teaches that man's spiritual relationship with God has been completely broken because of sin,
it does not see human nature as being so sinful that it cannot be cleansed and filled with the Holy Spirit in this life.
Sin's stranglehold on man can be ended.

> *Grace first contrived the way*
> *To save rebellious man;*
> *And all the steps that grace display*
> *Which drew the wondrous plan.*
> —DODDRIDGE

5

The Meaning and Nature of Sin

"Holiness is the symmetry of the soul"
(Philip Henry).

Adam's sin was both *disobedience* and *defiance* of God. His *actions* and his *spirit* were ungodlike, contrary to the divine holiness. As a result of Adam's sin, every man who comes into the world actually falls into sin, since he is depraved and corrupt. He does not live in the image of God. As a "child of wrath" he bears the image of his father—the devil (John 8:44). Not only does he sin, but he is sinful, turning away from God to self, to a false center or organizing principle of life (the primary meaning of "original" sin).

These two distinct understandings of sin run through the whole of Christendom. The word "sin" can be used either in the sense of *transgressing* a moral code, or in the sense of *rebellion* against God, and so being alien to Him.[1]

The meaning and nature of sin will be discussed in this chapter under two heads: (1) the dual nature of sin in Scripture, and (2) the Wesleyan understanding of sin.

THE DUAL NATURE OF SIN IN SCRIPTURE

This twofold understanding of sin is consistent with the teachings of the Bible. When used as a *verb*, the word "sin" suggests an act (sometimes an act of the mind), a deed, an overt transgression, as when Jesus said: "Neither do I condemn thee: go, and sin no more" (John 8:11). As a *noun* in the singular, "sin" usually indicates a condition of the soul. An example is Paul's usage in Rom. 6:12: "Let not sin [*hē hamartia*, literally, 'the sin,' the spirit of revolt, which issues in many transgressions] therefore reign in your mortal body, that ye should obey it in the lusts thereof."

Though sin is given many shades of meaning in the Scriptures, the Old and New Testaments support the claim that sin exists both as an *act* and as a *state* or *condition*.

A. Sin in the Old Testament

The Old Testament distinguishes deliberate acts of *transgression* (the breaking of prohibitions, as in the case of Adam and Eve in the Garden of Eden), sins of *ignorance* (including violations of the ceremonial law, which required sacrifice and atonement), and an inveterate *disposition of sinfulness* or *rebellion*. Sin was understood to be primarily against God and secondarily against man. Every sin against another person was regarded as against God, but not every sin against God (such as idolatry) was necessarily against man.

1. *Missing the Mark*

Many terms for "sinning" and "sin" are used in the Old Testament. Perhaps the most common word is *chatta*, which means "missing the mark" or "missing the way" (Prov. 8:36; 19:2). Depending on its use or context, the word may denote wrongs committed through negligence or ignorance, which required a sin offering (Lev. 4:13-14, 21) or deliberate sins and a sinful condition (Job. 1:22; Ps. 51:5, 9).

Since man was made originally in the image of God, he was intended to live as God lives. Therefore every departure from the law of God or from right was failure to fulfill this purpose, a missing of the moral goal of holiness.

2. *Violation of God's Commandments*

Abar is the Hebrew term used to designate the violation of a written commandment, whether deliberately or unwittingly. "To transgress" means to cross beyond a forbidden boundary into territory that is "out of bounds." A term similar in meaning, but including a more personal element, is the word *asham*. It went beyond infraction of an impersonal law and included failure to keep an agreement with another person. It is conveyed by the English word *breach*, as for example, Israel's breach of the covenant (Lev. 4:13; 5:2-3). The word *maal* conveys the idea of infidelity in marriage and also implies a breach of trust (Prov. 16:10).

3. *A Perverted Nature*

Awon (avah) is used in the Old Testament to indicate crookedness or perversion (Lam. 3:9*b*). It suggests wrong intention in an action or an omission that is not straight or not right. Though it conveys various meanings—"crime" or "iniquity," "guilt," "punishment"—several comparable contexts show that it means a distortion of the nature (1 Sam. 20:30; 2 Sam. 19:19; Prov. 12:8; Isa. 19:14; 21:3; Jer. 3:31; Lam. 3:9). It designates an evil disposition, both individual and corporate, which underlies specific acts of sin. The term provides strong support for the doctrine of original sin.

4. *Hostility to God*

Rasha, usually translated "wickedness," indicates a raging against God (Job 3:17; Ezek. 18:20-21; 33:8-9). This is one of the most common words for "sinner" in the Old Testament. It describes character, hostility to God, as well as individual actions.

Avel seems to suggest the idea of iniquity, though other renderings are given: "unjust" (Ps. 43:1; Prov. 29:27), "unrighteous" (Lev. 19:15; Deut. 25:16), "ungodly" (Job 16:11), "perverse" (Isa. 59:3), and "wicked" (Ps. 89:22).

Aven also is used frequently to express iniquity and is often connected with idolatry (Num. 23:21; 1 Sam. 15:23; Mic. 2:1). It has been translated as "unjust," "false," "mischief," "affliction," and "evil."

5. *A Spirit of Rebellion*

One of the stronger words for sin in the Old Testament is the term *pasha,* derived from a root meaning "to rebel" (1 Kings 12:19; Job 34:37). It refers to deliberate transgression, to a revolt or refusal to be subject to rightful authority (Gen. 50:17).

This was the favorite word of the eighth-century prophets, though it is frequently translated "transgressions." Amos declared that the *rebellions* of Judah are against the law of God (2:4). He complained that God's people had not ceased from their evil: "For I know how manifold are your rebellions and how mighty are your sins" (5:12). Hosea said that Israel behaved herself "like a *stubborn* heifer" (4:16, RSV). He spoke of "revolters" (5:2; 9:15), who have wandered away from God and rebelled against Him (7:13). Micah too spoke of the *"rebellion* of Jacob" and of the sons of Israel (1:5; 3:8). The same attitude is seen in Isaiah. His opening verse is: "I have nourished and brought up children, and they have *rebelled* against me" (1:2).

These four prophets were unanimous in viewing sin fundamentally as rebellion against God. They were thinking of a spirit, something much deeper than sin as a transgression against a law. Though they assumed that man can change his way of life if he will, they realized that man does not so will. They knew that his will is corrupt and impotent. Men are bound by their deeds, so that they cannot turn (Hos. 11:7). If ever there is any turning, God himself must turn them (Jer. 31:18).

Jeremiah asked why the migratory birds know the proper time to come back, but God's people do not know

(8:7). He preached that the people refused to know God because they had become "putrid" and "corrupt" (9:6). Hosea explained that "a spirit of whoredoms" had caused the people to go astray (4:12). By this he meant "that they are possessed by a *ruach* (spirit) which dominates their will, so that they are no longer able themselves to control their actions."[2]

6. *Stubbornness and an Inclination to Evil*

Several other words for sin as a condition are used in the Old Testament. One of them is *sheriruth*, usually translated "stubbornness" (Deut. 29:19; Jer. 3:17; 7:24; 9:14; 11:8; 12:10; 16:12; 18:12; 23:17). Perhaps the most significant word is *yetser hara* or "evil imagination" (Gen. 6:5; Deut. 31:21; 1 Chron. 28:9; Ps. 103:14; Isa. 29:16; Hab. 2:18). The term describes "the chronic evil inclination in mankind as a whole."[3] It strongly influenced the Christian writers of the New Testament.

One can scarcely deny that the Old Testament authors recognized the persistent sinful condition of the human race (Gen. 6:1 ff.) and of the nation of Israel (2 Kings 17:1 ff.; see also Isa. 6:5; Ps. 5; Ezek. 36:25-27). This concern with the inwardness of sin became increasingly prominent until the times of the New Testament, when it became the main preoccupation of the biblical writers.

It is apparent by the use of these Hebrew words that a twofold understanding of sin is found in the Old Testament. Sin is both an action—a failure to hit, or measure up to, God's standard of holiness; and an attitude of rebellion toward God and His authority, a condition of corruption.

B. Sin in the New Testament

1. *Pattern of Wickedness, Lawlessness*

Sin is viewed in the New Testament as unrighteousness *(adikia)*, translated variously as "unrighteousness"

(John 7:18; Rom. 1:18), "wickedness" (2 Thess. 2:12, NIV), and "iniquity" (James 3:6). It usually indicates a state or condition of wickedness, although occasionally it refers to doing "wrong" (2 Cor. 12:13).

Sin also is seen to be "lawlessness" *(anomia)*, frequently rendered "iniquity" (see Matt. 7:23*b*; 24:12). The term sometimes is contrasted with righteousness and holiness (Rom. 6:19*b*). First John 3:4 declares that all sin *(hamartia)* is lawlessness *(anomia)*. The term seems to refer to a pattern of conduct or spirit of rebellion against God.

The New Testament term for "rebellion" or "transgression" is *paraptōma,* also translated "trespasses" (Matt. 6:14; Mark 11:25). Basically the term denotes the sin of not knowing God and refers to the unregenerate.

2. *Willful Disobedience*

A similar term is *parabasis* ("transgression"), which means violation of a known rule, willful sin that brings guilt or condemnation. In terms of Adam's sin, it means disregard for God's law. Heb. 2:2 links the word with disobedience. *Parabasis* denotes not sins of ignorance but deliberate departures from the right (Rom. 4:15).

3. *Unbelief, Debauchery, and Self-assertion*

Apistia signifies unfaithfulness or unbelief. Unbelief may be a state of mind or an attitude toward God. Thus the writer of Hebrews speaks of the "evil heart of unbelief" (3:12). The term *aselgeia* indicates sin as debauchery, unbridled lust, licentiousness, shamelessness, etc. (Mark 7:21-22; Eph. 4:19; 2 Pet. 2:7). A condition of sin that permeates the entire personality is denoted.

Sin sometimes is viewed as desire *(epithymia,* which in itself is morally neutral) for that which is perverted or unlawful, as in Rom. 1:24, where it implies self-assertion over against the claims of God. Occasionally sin is described as irreverence or "ungodliness" *(asebeias,* 2 Tim. 2:16).

4. *Enmity, Opposition to God*

Paul spoke of sin as "enmity" *(echthra)*, which indicates active hatred toward God and opposition to Him (Rom. 8:7). It expresses man's strong determination to live apart from God and manage his own affairs. James also used the word to indicate antagonism or hostility to God (4:4).

5. *An Evil and Vicious Disposition*

The word *kakia* is a comprehensive term for opposition to virtue, or an evil disposition. The term means malignity, malice, ill will, desire to injure (Rom. 1:29; Eph. 4:31; Col. 3:8; Titus 3:3; James 1:21; 1 Pet. 2:1). It comes close to our term "depravity" (Acts 8:22; 1 Cor. 5:8; 14:20) and indicates a "maliciousness" that is not ashamed to break any law (1 Pet. 2:16). The term seems to imply a vicious disposition, the nature of character. *Ponēros* is used to indicate the positive expression of evil—that which is destructive and injurious (Mark 7:22; Luke 6:45).

6. *A Spirit of Sin*

The New Testament often singles out specific evil inclinations for condemnation, that is, a *spirit* of sin from which sins arise: "covetousness" (Rom. 7:8), "pride" (Luke 1:51; Rom. 1:30; 1 Cor. 4:6; 5:2; 8:1; 13:4), "selfishness" (Luke 16:19-31).

7. *A Condition of Sinfulness*

The New Testament vocabulary for sin contains 28 synonyms, derived from eight different roots. The one occurring most frequently is *hamart*. From it comes the most common verb for sin, *hamartanō* (*hamartia* is the noun), which means "to do wrong," "to trespass," "to sin against God." In classical Greek the term meant "to miss the mark," the equivalent of *chatta*, the Old Testament term. In the New Testament, however, it means more. It includes sin not only as an action *(hamartēma)* but also as a quality of action *(hamartia)*, referring to attitudes and responses (see Rom. 5:12; 6:12, 14; 7:20-21).

Hamartia appears more than 200 times in the New Testament, and of the 75 times it is used in the plural, it designates an act of sin. In the singular it denotes a principle or condition that needs cleansing or something more radical than forgiveness. After careful study of the use of the term, George Allen Turner observed:

> In the singular, . . . of approximately 125 occurrences only about 15 indicate sin as an act. In a small minority of instances—about 10 percent—*hamartia* in the singular and without the article designates an act of sin. In normal usage, therefore, this term without the article designates . . . a quality of sin or condition of sinfulness.[4]

8. *Sin as a Powerful Tyrant*

In most cases where *hamartia* is used in the singular with the definite article, it is personifying sin (see John 8:34; Heb. 3:13; 12:4; James 1:15). Particularly in the more than 20 occurrences of "sin" with the article *(hē hamartia)* in Rom. 5—8 (between 5:12 and 8:10), sin is referred to as a tyrant, as a force or principle underlying sinful acts, and not as a particular act of sin. Thus Dr. Turner, supported by other able scholars, has concluded:

> The evidence noted tends to confirm the generalization that *hamartia*, in the singular with the definite article, denotes the principle of sin which lies behind individual acts. Without the definite article this noun refers particularly to the quality, essence or nature of sin, the sinfulness of evil.[5]

This brief survey of the biblical terms used for sin indicates two primary meanings. Sin refers to actions that do not conform to God's standard. These actions may be deliberate or involuntary. However, the dominant emphasis of the biblical words is on *willful* actions. In addition, sin is a spirit of rebellion, of antagonism to God's will, purposes, and law—self-assertion as over against a holy God.

THE WESLEYAN UNDERSTANDING OF SIN

Wesleyan theologians have based their doctrine of a "second work of grace" in part on the biblical teaching of the twofold character of sin. While many words are used in Scripture to convey various shades of meaning with regard to it, the Bible does not give any formal definition of sin. John's statement that "sin is the transgression of the law" (1 John 3:4) may be the closest to such. It is incumbent upon us to take the biblical meanings and formulate an understanding of sin that is in harmony with the biblical teachings.

To define sin too broadly and label everything sin is in effect to make nothing sin and therefore would have little practical value. If sin is made to include every aspect of man's finite humanness, then deliverance from sin is impossible so long as the human remains. Deliverance from all sin in this life, however, is taught in the Scriptures.

A. Sins as Willful Transgressions

1. *Responsibility and Freedom*

Any understanding of sin—either actual sins or "in-being" sin—that removes man's responsibility is less than biblical. Because sin is a religious concept basically, and not merely an ethical one, man is accountable to God.

Accountability presupposes knowledge or awareness of the moral issues involved. Where there is ignorance, not due to willful blindness, any wrong act is an *error* and not sin in the strictest sense. Accountability presupposes some measure of freedom and some degree of involvement of the will. However, a sinful act need not be a premeditated one; it may be the result of earlier willing and conscious formation of habits, though the present action has become virtually unconscious.

2. Motives and Intentions

An adequate view of sin takes account of inner motives and intentions. The provision in the Old Testament sacrificial system for "sins of ignorance" (Lev. 4:13 ff., et al.) and the "cities of refuge" appointed by divine direction for the unintentional manslayer (Num. 35:6, 11 ff.) suggest that even during the regime of the Law, God made a distinction between unconscious and *conscious* or *willful* sins.

The New Testament is even more explicit in distinguishing mistakes and infirmities from sins. We are told that Jesus came to "save his people from [out of] their sins" (Matt. 1:21) and to "sanctify and cleanse" the Church (Eph. 5:25b-26a). He deals with sins and sin by forgiveness and cleansing (1 John 1:7), but He shares with humanity their infirmities (Heb. 4:15). Paul seems to have made the same distinction in his statement: "All *have sinned* [past tense], and all *do now come short* [present tense] of the glory of God" (Rom. 3:23, writer's paraphrase).

For this reason Wesley felt that the Bible regards only *voluntary* transgressions as sins. He wrote: "Nothing is sin, *strictly speaking*, but a voluntary transgression of a known law of God. Therefore, every voluntary breach of the law of love is sin; and nothing else, if we speak properly."

Wesley acknowledged that a "mistake is a transgression of the perfect law," but insisted, "This is not sin, if love is the sole principle of action." Nonetheless, both voluntary sins and involuntary mistakes need the atonement of Christ.[6] Only if sin is understood as a "voluntary breach of the law of love" could Wesley say that "a Christian can be perfect so as not to commit sin."

3. *The Legal and Ethical Definitions of Sin*

It is true that "sin" in its widest meaning refers to any falling short of the glory of God. The idea of missing the mark or falling below a divine standard is a biblical concept. Theologians call it the "objective" or "legal" view of sin. However, the primary biblical meaning of sin is that of willful, deliberate, premeditated transgression of, or disregard for, God's *known* law. It is designated as the "subjective" or "ethical" view of sin.

The former interpretation, generally held by Calvinistic thinkers, is expressed in the *Shorter Westminster Catechism:* Sin is "any want of conformity to or transgression of the law of God." This view seems to understand sin only as a matter of omissions and commissions, rather than a condition of the soul, analogous to disease in the body (see Mark 2:17).

4. *Inadequacy of the Legal View*

W. T. Purkiser has shown the inadequacy of this legal definition by examining the 41 verses in which the *verb* "to sin" *(hamartanō)* appears in the New Testament. He demonstrates that the definition cannot be substituted for the verb "to sin" without making the meaning ludicrous or warped. He gives the following example from the Gospels:

> In John 5:14 we read: "Afterward Jesus findeth him in the temple, and said unto him, Behold, thou art made whole: sin no more, lest a worse thing come unto thee." Let us substitute the legal definition. Then we would read: "Behold, thou art made whole: *deviate no more in any manner from an absolute standard of perfect behavior,* lest a worse thing come unto thee." This would certainly place the poor fellow in a terrible spot! How could he avoid all deviations from a perfect standard, known or unknown, voluntary or involuntary?[7]

To affirm the legal view of sin is to say that the essence of sin is in the act, not in the motive, intention, or knowledge prompting the act. If "sin is simply a deviation from rules, then righteousness is merely a matter of conformity to rules."[8] But this is contrary to everything that Jesus and the New Testament writers taught regarding the nature of sin and righteousness. Sin relates more to God himself, and His will for man, than to God's law as a set of rules for conduct.

5. *Practical and Biblical Character of the Ethical View*

Regardless of our doctrinal positions, in actual practice everybody lives by the ethical view of sin. The mother who, after many weeks of caring for her sick child, in her weariness one night gives the child the wrong medicine, resulting in his death, is not accounted a murderer, though the act itself is tragically wrong. She is to be comforted rather than accused. On the other hand, Jesus reminded us that one can be a murderer, though his spirit of murder never eventuates in an overt act of homicide.

Jesus taught that ethical sin brings God's judgment and condemnation (John 9:41). John takes the same position in his statement: "Whosoever abideth in him [Christ] sinneth not" (1 John 3:6-9). Obviously none could abide in Him—for this would be an impossible situation—if John meant unknown and involuntary transgressions and faults: "Whosoever abideth in him *makes no mistakes*."

With respect to God's absolute law, given to Adam prior to the Fall and requiring unqualified conformity, all men are transgressors.[9] Man's mental and bodily powers are so enfeebled that he inevitably falls into errors. Only Christ has fulfilled the Adamic law of innocence. Imperfection of knowledge may produce errors in judgment and consequent errors in conduct, but if these are without malice and confessed, God will not impute them to man. To sin ignorantly is to remain guiltless.

6. *Omissions and Guilt*

Man, however, is responsible for sins of omission. He

must confess and rectify them when they become known to him, although he is guilty of, or condemned for, only *willful* sins. Man becomes increasingly aware of his sin as he receives new light from God. This is consistent with the New Testament teaching that knowledge of sin comes by the law (Rom. 5:13; 7:7; also Gal. 3:19; 1 Tim. 1:9). This does not mean that until one is quickened, convicted, or made aware of his sin, he does not sin, understood in the broader sense. Rather, it means that before one is given the knowledge of the law, he is not guilty or condemned by God. All real guilt presupposes sin, but not all sin broadly conceived brings guilt or condemnation.

Whether the Christian who is made aware for the first time of some falling short experiences guilt is partly a semantic question—a problem of definition of terms. If by "guilt" is meant a deep sense of unworthiness and grief over an inadvertent or omitted action, then obviously the believer feels guilt. But if "guilt" connotes the condemnation of God, which disrupts and destroys fellowship, then he does not.

7. *Humanity and Sinfulness*

Any view of sin that makes humanity coequal with sinfulness, or that denies that sin in the "legal" sense may be present before one is aware of it, is faulty and unbiblical. There is no state of grace that excludes inadvertent transgressions. For these Jesus admonished His followers to pray for forgiveness (Matt. 6:12; 18:23 ff.; Luke 11:4; cf. 1 John 1:8-9). Every true believer heeds the tender correction of the Holy Spirit, senses his faults, seeks pardon for them, and presses on to the final mark. He does not grow self-defensive but acknowledges that moment by moment he lives on the basis of forgiveness.

Our failure to understand that the "saints" (the holy ones) are always less than they ought to be, or less than what

God yet has in mind for them, has often led to self-righteousness and spiritual pride among some, hypocrisy among others, and despair among the conscientious. The Holiness Movement has sometimes fostered a theology that will not permit confession or acknowledgment of falling below God's ultimate standard. This has drawn the criticism of W. E. Sangster, and others with him, that as a result, some have

> blunted their own conscience, believing that what they were doing was to the glory of God. When the inner monitor of the soul stirred in disapproval, they flung "a promise" at it, and called the warning "unbelief." With passing time the conscience ceased to function with any accuracy or power and they are found proclaiming themselves free of sin while guilty of conduct which a worldling would know to be wrong (W. E. Sangster, *The Path to Perfection* [London: Epworth Press, 1957], 139-40).

J. A. Wood, in his great holiness classic, *Perfect Love*, has similarly observed: "None see their need of the Atonement so clearly, or feel their need of its merits so deeply, as the *entirely* sanctified. He, more than any other man, feels, 'Every moment, Lord, I need the merit of Thy death.'" Deeply conscious of his faults, he pursues forgiveness for them and continues his Christian work. "Progress in saintliness always means at the same time progress in penitence," without a loss of confidence that one is accepted in the household of God.

Holiness theology steadfastly affirms that to insist that something is sin *only* if one believes it to be sin is less than scriptural. On the other hand an adequate theology of holiness refuses to define sin "properly so-called" as any lack of conformity to God's final standard. Holiness theology preserves the creative tension between deliverance from *willful* sin and a growing awareness of one's lack of *total conformity* to the "stature of the fulness of Christ" (Eph. 4:13). Without undermining the victory over sin promised by sanctifying grace, we freely acknowledge that even the most saintly Christians, "who feel nothing but love," still fall short of the glory of God and consequently need the Blood of Atonement (see Wesley's *Plain Account*, 81, 83).

Nonetheless, to be human is not to be a sinner in the primary biblical sense. Sin in its *fundamental* biblical meaning may result from willful transgression or from conscious failure to progress in holiness and the knowledge of God. The Christian enjoys a freedom from sinning, so that by this standard he does *not* sin every day in word, thought, and deed. He consequently is saved from the guilt and dominion of sin. Sin's reign over him is broken in the new birth by the power of grace.

B. Sin as Moral Corruption

Wesleyanism has never deviated from the doctrine of original sin, not only in the sense of Adam's primal transgression but also in the sense of a universal racial corruption of nature consequent to Adam's sin.

Augustine, in one strain of his thought, viewed original sin as concupiscence. Thus sin came to be seen by some as essentially a permanent, ineradicable impairment of the bodily nature from which man can be delivered only by death. The concept of the "sinful body" was buttressed by Luther and Calvin. But if original sin is so defined as to include inherited physical limitation as well as inherited moral depravity, then there can be no complete deliverance from it in this life.

1. *Moral Quality of Original Sin*

Some hold that Paul identified the physical body with sin and appeal to his statement in Rom. 7:18, "In me (that is, in my flesh [*sarx*]) dwelleth no good thing." Paul's usage varies. Occasionally "flesh" *(sarx)* is equivalent to the body *(soma)* (e.g., Rom. 2:28, 3:20; 4:1; 7:1; 1 Cor. 15:39, 50; Gal. 1:16). However, in most instances he used the term *sarx* in a moral rather than in a physical sense. Several categories of his "works of the flesh" are purely moral rather than physical (Gal. 5:19-23). He spoke of "strife and envying" as works of the "flesh" to be renounced (Rom. 13:13-14; 1 Cor. 3:3).

Paul contrasted "flesh" with "mind" and with Spirit (Rom. 7 and 8). Thus the "flesh" is the common enemy of the "mind" and the "Spirit of God." He could not have meant the body, because he insisted that the body is the shrine of the Holy Spirit (1 Cor. 3:16-17), and that members of the body be yielded to God as "instruments of righteousness" rather than as instruments of sin (Rom. 6:13; 12:1-2).

For Paul, the physical is neutral, but it will be controlled either by the "law of the flesh" or by the "law of the Spirit." "Flesh" *(sarx)*, with the definite article, is the source of all sorts of sin that seem to be present from birth (Gal. 5:16-25). To live "after the flesh" is to live for oneself, so that one's entire person—body, mind, and spirit—are under the power of sin (Rom. 8:5). While the body is the seat of sin, it is not sinful in itself. Thus deliverance from sin is not impossible while one is still "in the body."

Holiness literature sometimes refers to the sinful nature of man by using such terms as "principle," "principle of sin," "tendency to sin," "bias toward sin," and so on. These are descriptive rather than definitive, and thus are only partial. The biblical terms better convey the dynamic spiritual resistance to God that struggles against the Spirit.

2. *The Essence of In-being Sin*

What is this "indwelling" sin or "in-being" sin, "the sin" *(hē hamartia)* of which Paul spoke so graphically in

Rom. 5—8? This "original" sin is a spirit of willfulness, self-sovereignty, greed, revenge, and obstinacy. It is a false condition of egocentricity, a reliance upon one's own efforts to progress in the way of holiness, and a willingness to live independently of God—taking God for granted or presuming upon Him. This spirit is not the product of habit, inadequate education, or ill example. Rather, man reveals this spirit from his first conscious choice.

Richard Taylor identifies this sin nature

as a hard core of idolatrous self-love planted deep in the self as an inherited racial fault. We might call it a predispositional set toward idolatry—with self as the substitute god. When man fell, his life forces ceased to be oriented toward God and became oriented toward self. So fierce is this self-orientation that it creates a jealous, spontaneous resistance and resentment against anything that threatens the autonomy of self. The supreme threat is God; therefore He is the Object, even though more or less subconsciously, of the supreme aversion. Paul says that essentially this nature is "enmity against God; for it is not subject to the law of God, neither indeed can be" (Rom. 8:7). But its enmity is due to its self-idolatry—its carnal-mindedness—a *phroneo*, or disposition, which is set on the self and its interests.[10]

3. *The Dynamic Power of Indwelling Sin*

"In-being" sin is more than the sum total of sin's manifestations. It is a unitary principle, a deep state of enmity between the self-centered self and the claims of God. "Original" sin, however, is not a static substance, but a condition resulting from a disrupted divine-human relationship. Its power lies in its dynamic and personal character, which can be overcome and thwarted only by the greater power of divine love.

Augustine once wrote that no man can change the direction of his love any more than a rock can change the direction of its fall. This was his dramatic way of emphasizing the seriousness and tyrannical power of sin. Only the "expulsive power of a new affection"—the indwelling of the Holy Spirit (Rom. 8:9)—can drive out and replace self-love. This deep self-centeredness of man must and can be dealt with in a *radical instantaneous cleansing* of the wellsprings of the heart. Holiness theology claims that this moral crisis—*"entire sanctification"*—conforms to man's experience and is taught in Scripture as the glorious privilege of every truly regenerated child of God.

Man, made in the image of God, chose to make himself *in his own image.* He thereby forfeited his moral likeness and became a "child of wrath." However, through Christ's work on the Cross, there is provided for man deliverance from sin and self-centeredness.

> *We bless that wondrous purple stream,*
> *That cleanses every stain;*
> *Yet are our souls but half redeemed,*
> *If sin, the tyrant, reign.*
>
> *Lord, blast his empire with Thy breath;*
> *That cursed throne must fall.*
> *Ye flatt'ring plagues that work our death,*
> *Fly, for we hate you all.*
>   —ISAAC WATTS

6

Atonement:
The Possibility of Christlikeness

**"Holiness is not the way to Christ, but
Christ is the way to holiness."**

If man is to be accepted by a holy God, some means must
be made available to liberate him from his sinning and sinfulness, thereby bringing reconciliation, reclamation, and
restoration. God's Word proclaims that "the blood of Jesus
Christ . . . cleanseth . . . from *all* sin" (1 John 1:7). God's desire for a holy people is fulfilled by the work of His Son on
the Cross.

How the death of Christ breaks the power of sin and
brings new life may be beyond human comprehension.
That it does so, when the atoning benefits are appropriated
by faith, is the bold declaration of the Scriptures, Christian
faith, and experience.

Much preaching and teaching have failed to relate the
great biblical doctrines of holiness and sanctification to
Christ—His suffering, death, and resurrection. This may
explain in part why many misunderstand the holy life as
being one of intense stress and strain, mere human striv-
ing; or view entire sanctification as being optional in the
life of the believer.

The centrality of the Cross in bringing to fruition God's ultimate purpose is expressed eloquently by the apostle Paul:

> For what I received I passed on to you as of *first* importance: that Christ died for our sins according to the Scriptures, that he was buried, that he was raised . . . For I resolved to know nothing . . . except Jesus Christ and him crucified. . . . you are in Christ Jesus, who has become for us wisdom from God—that is, our righteousness, holiness and redemption *(1 Cor. 15:3-4; 2:2; 1:30, NIV)*.

Through God's reconciling love revealed in His Son at Calvary, the possibility of godlikeness, or Christlikeness, has been recovered. The *new covenant* has been established and *restoration to the image of God* has been initiated. "Therefore, if anyone is in Christ, he is a new creation; *the old has gone, the new has come!"* (2 Cor. 5:17, NIV).

In this redeeming work the whole Trinity is involved. It is accomplished by the Father (1 Thess. 4:3), by the Son (Heb. 13:12), and by the Holy Spirit (Rom. 15:16). Though the total being of God is active in every phase of redemption by which the Divine shares His holiness, for purposes of analysis we will discuss the redeeming activity of God under the following heads: (1) the Father's plan; (2) the Son's provision; and (3) the Spirit's proclamation.

THE FATHER'S PLAN

Divine initiative in solving man's sin problem is seen in the Cross, for "God was in Christ, reconciling the world unto himself" (2 Cor. 5:19). What was completed for us there was costly beyond reckoning and cannot be measured by material standards. "It was not with perishable things such as silver or gold that [we] were redeemed from the empty way of life handed down to [us] . . . but with the precious blood of Christ . . . He was chosen *before the creation of the world* . . . for [our] sake" (1 Pet. 1:18-20, NIV).

D. M. Baillie has expressed graphically the connection between God's eternal purpose and Christ's atonement: "There was a cross in the heart of God before there was one planted on the green hill outside of Jerusalem."[1] Atonement was not an afterthought. It was conceived and carried as a burden of love and a sacrifice of pain within the heart of God from eternity.

Whatever else may be said of God, He is not incapable of suffering. Even the "permission of moral evil in the decree of creation was at cost to God."[2] His suffering does not arise over a mere rejection of His love on the part of man, but out of man's flagrant disregard of God himself—His holy character. This is the patent implication of Paul's words: "He therefore that despiseth [the plan of holiness] despiseth not man, but God, who hath also given unto us his holy Spirit" (1 Thess. 4:8).

A. Weakness of the Law and Sacrifices

As shown in the Old Testament, the holiness of God was the basis for all His dealings with His people. Every statement of law, whether it referred to man's relationship to God or to man's relationship to man, arose out of God's holiness and His desire for holiness in men (see Exod. 20; Lev. 19). The Law demanded holiness. It stated: "Ye shall therefore keep my statutes, and my judgments: which if a man do, he shall live in them" (Lev. 18:5). However, man's sinfulness alienated him from the presence of a holy God and rendered him incapable of performing His holy commandments.

1. *Functions of the Law*

Divine law or commandments, though good and necessary, could not put away sin and effect a reconciliation between God and man. The Law was useful in *revealing* man's sin (Rom. 3:20) but was unable to *conquer* sin and restore the divine likeness. It revealed both God's requirements and man's inability to satisfy its demands.

2. *Precursors of Christ's Atonement*

The ceremonial law, with its sacrifices and sin offerings, provided a temporary means of atoning for transgressions of the primary covenant, namely, the Decalogue, or Ten Commandments (Gal. 3:19; Heb. 9:7). It served as a type of Christ (Col. 2:16-17) and taught the necessity of holiness and the shedding of blood as a means of remission for sin (Heb. 9:1-15).[3] While the sacrifices required by the Law had no power in themselves to atone for sin (cf. Heb. 10:1-4), they pointed forward in faith to the efficacy of Christ's sacrifice in fulfilling the demand of the Law.

3. *Essence of the Law*

Jesus simplified the divine commandments with His summary of the Decalogue: "Thou shalt love the Lord thy God with all thy heart, and with all thy soul, and with all thy mind. . . . And the second is like unto it, Thou shalt love thy neighbour as thyself. On these two commandments hang all the law and the prophets" (Matt. 22:37, 39-40). Thus complete or perfect love for God and man would satisfy God's demand for holiness.

However, Jesus "knew what was in man" (John 2:25), that man of himself could not love as God required. Therefore this requirement was linked with the new life-giving power to accomplish it that He came to impart. Holiness would be possible by the enablement derived from "being in Christ," the "second Adam" or "new Man."

4. *The New Covenant and the Atonement*

Christ's atonement established the "new covenant" of personal holiness and righteousness spoken of in Luke 1:72-75:

> To show mercy to our fathers
>   and to remember his holy covenant,
>   the oath he swore to our father Abraham:
> to rescue us from the hand of our enemies,
>   and to *enable us* to serve him without fear
>   in holiness and righteousness before him *all*
>   *our days (NIV).*

Neither Christ's death nor His teachings annulled the primary old covenant (Ten Commandments) but made adherence to them a possibility as had been promised: "I will put my laws into their minds, and write them in their hearts" (Heb. 8:10). "The standards of right and wrong are not changed to fit man's nature, but man's nature is changed to fit those standards. In this sense, he is freed from the [condemnation of] the law."[4]

5. *Fulfillment of the Law*

Paul related the weakness of the Law to its fulfillment by Christ and the consequent empowering of the believer that that fulfillment brings when appropriated by faith:

> For the law of the Spirit of life in Christ Jesus hath made me free from the law of sin and death. For what the law could not do, in that it was weak through the flesh, God sending his own Son in the likeness of sinful flesh, and for sin, condemned sin in the flesh: that the righteousness [ordinances, or requirements] of the law might be fulfilled *in us*, who walk not after the flesh, but after the Spirit *(Rom. 8:2-4).*

Through Christ's atoning work the old ceremonial sacrifices were replaced with "a more excellent ministry" and a "better covenant . . . established upon better promises" (Heb. 8:6).

The ceremonial law and sacrifices gave way to grace, "whereby God . . . redeems man and conforms . . . [his] nature to the whole will and nature of God, by *free pardon and sanctification*, through simple faith in the blood of Christ and by the direct agency of the Holy Spirit." Grace is not merely the unmerited *favor of God toward man* but also an imparted ability from God to man, enabling him to measure up to the divine standard of holiness and righteousness.[5]

> *To see the law by Christ fulfill'd,*
> *And hear His pardoning voice,*
> *Changes a slave into a child,*
> *And duty into choice.*
>   —WILLIAM COWPER

B. God's Love and the Cross

1. *Divine Judgment and the Remission of Sins*

The Cross reveals God's judgment on sin arising out of His holiness, and His forbearance in the remission of sins arising out of His love. The classic biblical statement combining these truths is given by Paul:

> God presented [Jesus] as a sacrifice of atonement, through faith in his blood. He did this to demonstrate his justice, because in his forbearance he had left the sins committed beforehand unpunished—he did it to demonstrate his justice at the present time, so as to be just and the one who justifies those who have faith in Jesus *(Rom. 3:25-26, NIV)*.

In order that God's holiness would not be compromised by His offer of justification (forgiveness or pardon) and sanctification, He bore the penalty for our sin by His Son. Here is the supreme paradox of the Christian faith— God himself in Christ paid the cost of our sins!

2. *A God of Holy Love*

God is not only holy in character but also loving in nature. The relation of God's holiness and love has been stated thus:

Holiness furnishes the norm for love and therefore must be superior [i.e., logically antecedent] to it. God is not holy because He loves, but loves because He is holy. . . . Both holiness and love belong to the divine essence . . . and cannot be separated except in thought. Justice, therefore, can never be necessary and mercy optional, but are always conjoined; and in the redemptive economy, holiness and mercy are supreme.[6]

God's holiness and love are in no way opposed. What His holiness demands, His love provides (1 Pet. 3:18). The motive for the Atonement is found in the love of God, and Christ's life and death are expressions of that love.

For God so loved the world that he gave his one and only Son . . . to save the world through him. . . . But God demonstrates his own love for us in this: While we were still sinners, Christ died for us. . . . This is how God showed his love among us: He sent his one and only Son into the world that we might live through him. . . . If God is for us, who can be against us? He who did not spare his own Son, but gave him up for us all—how will he not also, along with him, graciously give us all things? *(John 3:16-17; Rom. 5:8; 1 John 4:9; Rom. 8:31-32, NIV).*

Christ is not One who by His death and intercession *spares* man the wrath of the Father. He is the One who freely *carries out* the will of the Father. At Calvary, "mercy and truth are met together; righteousness and peace have kissed each other" (Ps. 85:10).

THE SON'S PROVISION

The occasion for the Atonement, God's offering up of Christ as the "propitiation for our sins" (1 John 2:2; 4:10; cf. Rom. 3:25), is the presence in the world of sinfulness (original sin) and actual sins. By His death and resurrection

Christ has defeated the powers of evil (Col. 2:13-15); has slain the enmity between man and God and between man and man (Rom. 5:11; 2 Cor. 5:18-19; Eph. 2:14-16); and has opened the fountain of sanctification for mankind, making possible a life of victory over sin and day-to-day holy living (Eph. 5:25-27; Heb. 13:12; 1 John 1:7).

This "free gift" is extended to all who will believe (Rom. 5:18). Accepting the provisions that God's holiness and love bestow brings the victory described by Paul: "But now being made free from sin, and become servants to God, ye have your fruit unto holiness, and the end everlasting life" (Rom. 6:22).

To be reconciled to God is to avail oneself, through faith in Christ, of the benefits of the Atonement, by which we are delivered from *(a)* the *guilt* of sin; *(b)* the *reigning power* of sin; and *(c)* the *in-being* of sin.

The first occurs in justification and adoption; the second in regeneration (which is simultaneous with justification and with it constitutes conversion or the new birth); and the third in entire sanctification (which we believe is a "second" work of grace "subsequent to regeneration"). Christ's atonement is the means by which reconciliation or "at-one-ment" with God becomes reality.

A. At-one-ment of Fellowship

1. *Justification*

To be justified is to be forgiven of all *past* sins by the gracious act of God, freed from the condemnation or guilt of sin, and accepted before God as though one had never sinned. Justification is what God has done *for* us in Christ. It effects a change of relationship to God, who declares one to be righteous. However, God never *declares* one righteous (justified) without *making* him righteous. For God to do so would be for Him to err or lie.

2. *Adoption*

Like justification, adoption is an act of God that takes place apart from us and describes a change in our relation to Him. "By justification, God takes us into His favor; by adoption, into His heart."[7] Whereas justification overcomes alienation and enmity, adoption brings one into the family and affection of God.

The blessings and rights of the adopted are many. If one is a child, then he is an "heir of God, and joint-heir with Christ" (Rom. 8:17). As a son, one has a proprietary claim to all that Christ has and is. "All things are yours" (1 Cor. 3:21). And, of course, there is the title to an eternal inheritance (2 Tim. 4:8; James 1:12; 1 Pet. 1:4).

> *Behold, what wondrous grace*
> *The Father hath bestow'd*
> *On sinners of a mortal race,*
> *To call them sons of God!*
> —Isaac Watts

B. At-one-ment of Character

Marvelous as is the new relationship described by justification and adoption, it falls far short of the full benefits of the Atonement. They have to do with a reconciliation or "at-one-ment" of *fellowship* with God. In light of the intransigent character of sin and God's desire for holiness in man, there must also be possible an "at-one-ment" of *character*. Thus we are admonished to "put off the old man" and "put on *the new man, which after God is created in righteousness and true holiness*" (Eph. 4:22-24; cf. Rom. 13:14; Col. 3:9-10).

The Atonement provides more than forgiveness of sins and adoption into the family of God. "The main thing in man's salvation is not the removal of guilt, but the actual transformation of a sinner into an obedient child of God."[8]

1. *Union with Christ*

Salvation involves a positive as well as a negative aspect. In conversion the negative aspect is pardon, justification. But positively, God proposes to give of himself and to make us "like Christ." Christ's death on the Cross not only is "for us" but also is God's means of working "in us." "Christ *in you*, the hope of glory" (Col. 1:27).

The divine life is to flow through God's people as the life of the vine flows through the branches (John 15:1 ff.). That He may reproduce His own life in us is the purpose of His coming and of the gift of the Spirit. "I am come that they might have life, and that they might have it more abundantly" (John 10:10). Christ took our death; but we must take His life!

The positive side of one's conversion is *regeneration*, the impartation of the life of God to the soul (John 5:21). There are no degrees of justification. One is either pardoned, or he is not. In this sense, it is full, perfect, and complete. But with regeneration or "life in Christ," the "new man" (2 Cor. 5:17) begins—to be followed by increasing conformity to His likeness.

Atonement is more than the breaking of the barrier of sin, more than an end to the separation that sin has brought. By Christ's death we are incorporated into His spiritual Body, the Church. There is a "new, organic spiritual union with Christ, so that we are, in a sense that utterly surpasses knowledge, at one with him."[9]

2. *Sanctification Through Christ*

Christ "in us" is our "sanctification [holiness]" (1 Cor. 1:30). James Stewart emphasizes the relationship between at-one-ment with Christ and our sanctification—the positive side of our salvation: "Only when union with Christ is kept central is sanctification seen in its true nature, as the unfolding of Christ's own character within the believer's life; and only then can the essential relationship between religion and ethics be understood."[10]

The purpose of all sanctification is to break the power and dominion of sin, to remove the condition of sin that is self-idolatry and self-centeredness, and to refashion us in Christ's likeness. Through the Atonement reconciliation—of both fellowship and character—is possible. By it "our sinful self-seeking is overcome and fellowship with God is created in which it is replaced by living for Christ."[11]

Sanctification in the fullest biblical sense denotes the *complete* recovery, by grace, from the effects of sin. The fact that all of these are not removed immediately, but progressively and in distinct stages, in no way suggests a limitation of God's power. Rather, it relates to man's capacity to respond to God's grace.[12]

All holiness and sanctification are the result of God's activity in Christ on the Cross. As stated in Part I (p. 17), the terms "holiness" and "sanctification" do not have the same meaning. "Holiness," as it relates to man, refers to holy living, to the quality and stages of one's moral or religious life; "sanctification" denotes the act or process by which one is made holy.[13]

Scripture distinguishes three meanings of sanctification, each of which is God's work, and by which man is made holy.[14]

a. *Continuing sanctification—a total process.* The word *hagiasmos* (accurately translated "sanctification" in most cases in ASV, NASB, and RSV) occurs numerous times in the New Testament and signifies progress (see Rom. 6:19, 22; 1 Cor. 1:30; 1 Thess. 4:3-4, 7; 2 Thess. 2:13; 1 Tim. 2:15; Heb. 12:14; 1 Pet. 1:2). It refers to the total work of God from the first moment of conviction (spiritual awakening) to the final "conformity" (if we may properly speak of "final") to the image of Christ. Nowhere is this power for holy living or growth *within* grace (not growth "into" grace) understood to be the consequence of mere human effort. "Perfecting holiness in the fear of God" in all the aspects of daily life (2 Cor. 7:1; Heb. 6:1) always presupposes the divine activity.

  b. Initial sanctification (1 Cor. 6:9-11). This is the washing from the inward *guilt* of sin—the washing of regeneration. It is the cleansing of the sinner from his old sins, from the uncleanness that accompanied his sinful deeds. All believers are washed from their sins, delivered from the dominion or *power* of sin. Initial sanctification occurs simultaneously with the new birth or regeneration and continues throughout the Christian life until we see Christ face-to-face.

  A decisive transition is made in the moment of conversion, at which time every Christian is initially "sanctified" or made "holy" (literally, "holified"). The true Christian enjoying continuing sanctification seeks to live out this "new relationship" and, under the tender tutelage of the Holy Spirit, moves normally to the next critical stage of Christian development in the life of holiness—entire sanctification and beyond.

  c. Entire sanctification. By faith, in a *moment,* the believer is cleansed from the in-being or pollution of sin, and the heart is perfected in love (see John 17:17-19; 2 Cor. 7:1; Eph. 1:4; 5:26; 1 Thess. 5:23-24). Here God's work, begun in regeneration and even before, finds completion in a "bond of perfectness" that ties the Christian equally with God and neighbor.

  One who is born of the Spirit cannot oppose this divine cleansing or draw back from the ultimate goal of Christlikeness. He may wait for more light—being obedient as he does so. There may be a temporary reluctance to move on to entire sanctification once he sees clearly the implications of his initial commitment; but he cannot stubbornly resist and at the same time be worthy of his "high calling of God in Christ Jesus" (Phil. 3:14).

It is a mistake to limit our understanding of the Atonement to man's justification. It encompasses man's sanctification as well, including cleansing from all sin, the infilling of the Holy Spirit, and moment-by-moment union with Christ. Ralph Earle states it simply: "The sanctified life is the Christ life . . . if his [Christ's] full surrender was the procuring cause of our Atonement, our full surrender [yielding up of the self-life] is the means by which it is made effective in us."[15]

How this provisional at-one-ment becomes operative in us by the work of the Holy Spirit we must attempt to show from the Scriptures.

THE SPIRIT'S PROCLAMATION

The connection between redemption through Christ and the sanctifying work of the Holy Spirit is dramatized in Jesus' words: "He shall glorify me: for he shall take of mine, and shall shew it unto you" (John 16:14). The Holy Spirit makes real or actual within the believer what Christ accomplished by His suffering, death, and resurrection. Paul stated it thus in 1 Cor. 6:11: "But you were washed, you were sanctified, you were justified in the name of the Lord Jesus Christ and by the Spirit of our God" (NIV).

A. Newness of Life

1. *The Gift of the Holy Spirit*

The Holy Spirit is the Agent of our new life or new birth (John 3:1-15). Hence He is called the "Spirit of life," freeing us from sin's death (Rom. 8:2). The Christian begins his walk with God by the Spirit, as shown in Paul's challenge to the Galatians: "Are you so foolish? After begin-

ning with the Spirit, are you now trying to attain your goal
by human effort?" (3:3, NIV).

The New Testament explicitly states that the converted man receives and possesses the Holy Spirit. In the classic justification passage (Rom. 5:1-5) Paul stated that "God
has poured out his love into our hearts by the Holy Spirit,
whom he has given us" (v. 5, NIV). He spoke of the Spirit
as "the Spirit of Christ" and declared, "If anyone does not
have the Spirit of Christ, he does not belong to Christ" (8:9,
NIV). Although every believer possesses the Holy Spirit, it
does not follow that the Holy Spirit possesses or fully controls every believer.

It is not incorrect to say that "the paramount burden
of the Pauline Epistles is the sanctification of the Church."[16]
Paul's doctrine of sanctification is set forth in Rom. 5—8.[17]
He taught that by union with the crucified-resurrected
Christ we receive the life-giving Spirit. The Spirit dwells
within the believer as the sanctifying Spirit of Christ. The
Christian does not live "in the flesh" but "in the Spirit"
(8:9; Gal. 5:25), who becomes the pledge or guarantee of
our final resurrection with Christ (Rom. 5:15; 8:18; 2 Cor.
1:21-22; Eph. 1:13-14).

The believer's life in the Spirit, then, embraces his existence in Christ from justification to glorification. Here is
the New Testament basis for a doctrine of progressive or
continuing sanctification, which includes the distinct moments of justification and regeneration, entire sanctification, and finally, glorification at the last day.[18]

2. *The Beginning of Sanctification*

As we have seen, the believer's sanctification (or life
of holiness) begins at his conversion. By an act of faith he
accepts the fact that in the cross of Christ he has died to sin
(Rom. 6:1-2). The clear meaning is that the power of sin is
broken; one ceases to sin and comes under the greater

power of grace. The sin-controlled self, our "old man," has been "crucified" with Christ (Rom. 6:6; Gal. 5:24).

The Holy Spirit through the Word shows what Christ has done in our behalf. "He appeared so that he might take away our sins" (1 John 3:5, NIV) and "He himself bore our sins in his body on the tree, so that we might die to sins and live for righteousness" (1 Pet. 2:24, NIV). By His death on the Cross, Christ not only took upon himself the stroke due us but also bore *us* to the Cross. He died both as our Substitute and as our Representative. Thus Paul declared: "One died for all, and therefore all died . . . that those who live should no longer live for themselves but for him" (2 Cor. 5:14-15, NIV).

Just as by faith the believer is identified with Christ's death, so also by faith he is identified with Christ's resurrection. The believer has also "been raised up from the dead [the grave of trespasses and sins] by the glory of the Father . . . [to] walk in newness of life" (Rom. 6:4).

This "newness of life" is described as "new life of the Spirit" (Rom. 7:6, RSV), walking *"according* to the Spirit" (8:4, NIV), and being "led by the Spirit" (v. 14). This is the new birth spoken of by Jesus (John 3:3-8). It is to become "a new creature" in Christ Jesus; "old things . . . [have] passed away; behold, all things . . . [have] become new" (2 Cor. 5:17). This is the beginning of both *outward* and *inward* sanctification.

B. Life in the Spirit

1. *Believers Are to Go On to Entire Sanctification*

The sanctification that begins with conversion is not to be confused with *entire* sanctification for obvious reasons:

a. Christian believers are sometimes referred to as being "yet carnal" (1 Cor. 3:1-4) and therefore possessing am imperfect faith (1 Thess. 3:10; 4:3-8; 5:23). Paul prayed that they would be sanctified "wholly" (1 Thess. 5:23).

b. The apostle admonished believers to "reckon" or

consider themselves "to be dead indeed unto sin, but alive unto God through Jesus Christ our Lord" (Rom. 6:11); and therefore to "yield [themselves] to God as men who have been brought from death to life, and [their] members to God as instruments of righteousness" (Rom. 6:13, RSV).

2. *Complete Consecration Is a Condition*
   for Entire Sanctification

The word "yield" is expressed by the aorist tense, which suggests a specific act of "unconditioned submission to the Lordship of Christ." This is the moment or "crisis" of entire sanctification, in which the sinful nature is expunged from the heart.

T. A. Hegre comments on the nature of the critical and complete yielding up to God: "Surrender is the denial of self—not the denial of things, and not even self-denial (so-called). Denial of self is an utter unconditional surrender [not abject capitulation] to Jesus Christ, including the giving up of all my 'rights to myself.'"[19]

As Adam ceased to be God-centered and through sin became self-centered, so also are those who are "in Adam." They are slaves to Satan. The essence of man's sin is his "own-wayness," the substitution of his way for God's way. This nature of sin must be dealt with in a radical identification with Christ's death and resurrection. Only thus can one be transformed so as to bear His likeness.

3. *Entire Sanctification Is More than Consecration*

Consecration is a human work, though possible only by grace; entire sanctification is a divine work. This act of God by His Spirit within the believer corresponds with "perfecting holiness" (2 Cor. 7:1); with being "sanctified wholly" (*holoteleis*), entirely and perfectly (1 Thess. 5:23); with being "filled with the Spirit" (Eph. 5:18; also 3:14-20); and being made "blameless in love" (Eph. 1:4; 5:25-27; 1 Thess. 3:13).

Jesus clearly taught the conditions for making His

atonement effective in us personally. He said: "Whosoever will come after me, let him *deny himself,* and *take up* his cross, and *follow* me" (Mark 8:34). The words "deny" and "take up" are in the aorist tense, indicating a definite crisis, a specific point in time. The word "follow," however, is in the continuous present tense, meaning, "keep on following me," and indicating the progressively unfolding nature of consecration and sanctification.

4. *The Life of Holiness Involves Continuous Submission to Christ*

Following Christ daily includes bringing our bodies into full subjection to God. The body is not sinful but has been under "bad management." Now the body must be disciplined and sacrificed, if necessary, for the glory of God and the good of others. Jesus spoke of handing over the new life to God so that it may bring forth fruit (John 12:24), and Paul admonished believers to "present [their] bodies a living sacrifice . . . unto God" (Rom. 12:1).

The continuing life of holiness, or the progressive aspect of sanctification, is indicated by the present tense used in Rom. 6:16: "Don't you know that when you offer yourselves to someone to obey him as slaves, you are slaves to the one whom you obey—whether you are slaves to sin, which leads to death, or to obedience, which leads to righteousness?" (NIV). Regarding this continuing life in the Spirit, W. M. Greathouse has observed:

> The "yielded" life is a life put at God's disposal "moment by moment . . ." This is what Wesley, after Jesus, calls "abiding in Christ," and what Paul means by "walking by [better "in," that is, not merely "according to" or "in conformity with"] the Spirit."[20]

CONCLUSION

Adam's sin corrupted the entire human race. It affected man's relationship toward his *Sovereign*—and brought alienation and spiritual death; it affected man's relationship with his own *self*—and brought guilt, condemnation, and corruption; it affected his relationship to *Satan*—and brought enslavement and loss of spiritual freedom; it affected his relationship to *society*—and brought injustice and unrighteousness among men and nations.

These fundamental human problems have been solved in Christ's atonement. God's magnificent plan of redemption carried out on Calvary reestablished the relationship with God—and brings reconciliation, adoption into the family of God, and new life; it recovers the true self—and brings forgiveness, acceptance, and cleansing; it breaks the power of Satan and restores the God-given ability or freedom to love; it makes possible harmony between various segments of society, peace with one's fellows, and continued growth in Christian character.

To these ends "Jesus . . . suffered outside the city gate to make the people holy through his own blood" (Heb. 13:12, NIV). And "our old man was crucified with him, that the body of sin might be destroyed, that henceforth we should not serve sin" (Rom. 6:6). "Thanks be to God! He gives us the victory through our Lord Jesus Christ" (1 Cor. 15:57, NIV).

> *Amazing goodness! love divine!*
> *O may our grateful hearts adore*
> *The matchless grace; nor yield to sin,*
> *Nor wear its cruel fetters more.*
> —DANIEL STEELE

| 7 |

Common Misunderstandings and Questions

"A holy life is not an ascetic, or gloomy, or solitary life, but a life regulated by divine truth and faithful in Christian duty. It is living *above* the world while we are still *in* it" (Tryon Edwards).

Throughout its history the Christian Church has declared that sanctification in its fullest sense is a process of moral and spiritual renewal beginning with regeneration and continuing to glorification. We believe as our "distinguishing" doctrine that within the process of the believer's renewal in the image of God there is a distinct critical moment when he is baptized with the Holy Spirit and cleansed from the "in-being" sin—"entire," as distinct from "initial," sanctification (1 Thess. 5:23, NASB).

The first work of the devil in the Garden of Eden was to produce a state of *alienation* from God and *rebellion* against Him. However, "the reason the Son of God appeared was to destroy the devil's work" (1 John 3:8, NIV).

Therefore, redemption is totally adequate to meet man's spiritual need. The atonement of Christ deals not only with the *manifestations* of sin but with the *condition* of sin; not only with the symptoms but with the disease.

UNFORTUNATE MISUNDERSTANDINGS

This doctrine has sometimes been discredited by faulty misunderstandings, even by those who espouse its truth. It is imperative that these errors be exposed and removed. Otherwise the clear biblical teaching will be blurred, and many Christians will be hindered from entering into the "rest" provided for them (Heb. 4:9). We will note some of the more common misunderstandings.

A. That External Signs Are Sufficient Criteria for Judging One's Christian Experience, Especially Entire Sanctification

External standards of various kinds frequently have been held up as a necessary evidence that one has been entirely sanctified. Where certain preconceived conditions have not appeared, individuals have been judged as not having entered this state of grace. Various modes of dress, prescribed emotional reactions under severe stress, display of a particular gift of the Spirit, have all at one time or another been cited as the sign that one is indeed "sanctified wholly," or filled with the Spirit.

1. *The Limitation of Human Standards*

Such standards overlook the fact that one's habits of dress may be determined as much by financial resources or personal taste as by desire for modesty; that some people are sweeter or more poised by natural endowment or temperament than by grace; and that Scripture gives the *fruit* of the Spirit as part of the evidence of sanctification rather than any given *gift* of the Spirit. Furthermore, they fail to see that God deals with each person individually, and the degree of light given is not always the same for everyone at a given point in time.

2. *The Virtues of Christ Must Be Manifest*

It is true that "by their fruits ye shall know them" (Matt. 7:20). However, mere *human* standards of measurement are unbiblical and inadequate. Rather, the Spirit (virtues) of Christ must be evident. Even with this standard it is not always possible to be certain regarding another's spiritual status. Jesus' admonition is applicable here: "Judge not, that ye be not judged" (v. 1).

This is not to suggest that Christian modesty of dress is unimportant—indeed, the Christian's lifestyle is markedly different from that of the unbeliever; or that the Spirit does not assist in dealing with emotional and temperamental problems; or that the gifts of the Spirit are insignificant. It is to say that Christlikeness, divine love lived out through us, ultimately is the only firm standard of measurement. And Christ is to do the measuring, rather than His followers.

B. That the Believer Who Is Not Yet Sanctified Wholly Has Not Received the Holy Spirit

Because the spirit of sin, a spirit of selfishness, technically called "original sin," remains within the converted person until abolished in entire sanctification, some have reasoned that one cannot receive the Holy Spirit until that moment, since—according to their premise—the Holy Spirit will not reside in a heart where there is yet sin.

1. *No Known Sin Is Tolerated by Any Christian*

This conclusion overlooks the fact that the true Christian willingly condones no conscious sins or sin. Both are personal and involve a faulty relationship to God. Therefore a personal analogy may shed light on this misunderstanding.

Two persons may be getting to know one another, and yet one of them may be keeping himself *unconsciously* from the other—he is not completely open. The relationship is nonetheless fruitful and rewarding. However, when he becomes *conscious* of this reservation, he must open himself to the other person, or the relationship will be disrupted and broken off.

This is analogous to the life and experience of the Christian not yet *entirely* sanctified. He truly feels at his conversion that the submission of his sovereignty to God is complete, that the spirit of sin surely has been removed. Not until later is he made aware of an inward reservation that protects the self.[1] It is the regenerating Spirit who enables the believer to deal with this now conscious reservation.

2. *The Indwelling of the Spirit Is a Mark of the*
   New Covenant

Dr. G. B. Williamson wrote: "Those who affirm that there is no measure of the Holy Spirit imparted to a regenerate Christian are without scripture to support their view."[2] Scripture is clear (as seen in chapter 6) in its teaching that the Holy Spirit comes to reside in the believer at his conversion. God places His Spirit, the Spirit of Christ, within His own. This is a mark of the new covenant. (See John 6:56; 14:17, 20; 15:4; 17:26; Rom. 8:9; 1 Cor. 3:16-17; 6:19; 2 Cor. 13:5; 1 John 3:24; 4:4, 12-13, 15.)

To be converted to Christ (saved) is to receive the Holy Spirit: "If any man have not the Spirit of Christ, he is none of his" (Rom. 8:9). "No one can say, 'Jesus is Lord,' except by the Holy Spirit" (1 Cor. 12:3, NIV). Every person who has become a new creature in Christ has received the Holy Spirit.

It has been stated that in regeneration the Spirit of Christ becomes resident within the believer, whereas in entire sanctification He becomes president, or in full control of one's life. In the former, the Spirit sometimes goads, illuminates, and prods into activity; in the latter, He guides, invigorates, and penetrates every activity.[3]

C. That the Believer Receives Only a Part of the Holy Spirit

Others do not deny the reception of the Holy Spirit in conversion but imagine that the believer receives only a *part* of the Holy Spirit in the initial work of grace and the balance, or another part, when one is *entirely* sanctified.

1. *Love Requires Total Commitment*

This view embodies a quantitative figure and thus is misleading. Since God is a Person who desires to give of himself, and we are persons who were made to share His likeness, a personal analogy may be better. Consider the relationship of love between a young man and woman. Their romance may reach such a stage that "engagement" is appropriate—a "crisis" involving distinct and critical vows to each other. This we may liken to conversion.

In a normal relationship this commitment will develop to the decisive and transitional moment of marriage, in which each *completely* yields his or her life to the other. Each thought he or she had given all at the time of engagement; but standing before the altar, each one sees more involved now than before. Yet with eyes open, each commits himself or herself unreservedly. This may be analogous to *entire sanctification*.

Then comes actual life in marriage in which new situations arise and new sacrifices are made. But the once-for-all commitment is not up for review. This parallels the continuing and progressive life of the entirely sanctified.

Further, the relationship becomes increasingly deeper. It would be less than adequate to say that these young persons receive *one part* of each other at one stage and the remainder at a later stage—if by these terms we refer to a quantitative entity. Rather, we say that they come "to know"—love, appreciate, understand—each other progressively better. They are increasingly "comfortable" in the presence of the other and progressively assured of the other's approval—without taking the other for granted. In no way does this minimize the distinctive "crises" of engagement and marriage.

2. *God's Love Compels Him to Give All of Himself*

The analogy is a biblical one used again and again to describe the spiritual life in relation to God. God initiates a romance with man through prevenient grace. In the offer of himself He gives all! He does not give a part of himself to one, and reserve a different fragment for another, or for the same person to be given later. God is not an infinite philanthropist who in every gift withholds more than He has bestowed. He gives all of himself at any given moment, though men's capacities and abilities to appropriate vary according to their stage of spiritual development.

When men respond obediently, there is an *engagement* —the crisis of new birth occurs. As the romance deepens, the believer comes to see what this engagement means— the *total* giving and renunciation of oneself. One may have thought this problem of self was solved, but the growing relationship shows otherwise. Thus he or she is drawn to the *second crisis* of *entire sanctification,* in which he or she submits to the full implications involved.

Then comes the *life* of "Christian perfection," full Christian holiness, which must be lived moment by moment. New situations will arise and further decisions will be called for, but the fundamental and critical commitment does not require reconsideration. A call to special ministry, for example, is not a crisis in the sense of deciding *whether* to do God's will—though it may be critical regarding *what* is God's will. Like marriage, this divine-human love affair becomes increasingly rich and full.

D. That Original Sin Is a Thing

It is impossible to define "original" sin with satisfying accuracy. Even the writers of the Scriptures, divinely inspired as they were, were forced to accommodate their truths to the limitations of human speech. As a consequence, the Word of God refers to the sin of man's heart as "the body of sin" (Rom. 6:6), or "the body of this death" (7:24). Such figures fall short of a full understanding, since they are but symbols descriptive of a moral condition.

1. *Sin Is a Moral Quality*

Failing to understand this limitation and function of language, many have given a literalistic interpretation to the figures of speech describing sin. As a consequence, too many either have rejected the possibility of cleansing from all sin or have been seriously, but needlessly, perplexed as to how sin can be removed from the heart; or how, once removed, "it" could ever return to pollute man's inner being. H. V. Miller has given us a needed word of caution:

> Sin is not a SOMETHING. It is not an actual SUBSTANCE. Sin is a moral quality. Too often even those who have personally experienced heart purity have been puzzled as to what the sin of the heart actually is. Sin is a virus in the bloodstream of the moral nature; . . . a malignancy moving within the moral nature of man. But we must again caution ourselves to remember the fact that it is not an actual substance.[4]

2. *Sin Is a Condition, Not an Unchanging State*

J. B. Chapman likened "original" sin to darkness, adding that the Spirit's presence in our lives is analogous to the light that expels it. Thus he thought it more profitable to think of the *condition* rather than the *state* of holiness.[5] John put it clearly: "If we walk in the light, as he is in the light, we have fellowship one with another, and the blood of Jesus Christ his Son cleanseth us from all sin" (1 John 1:7).

Because "original" sin is not a material entity, which in that case could never return once its "roots" were destroyed, the cleansing that occurs in a *moment* must continue moment by moment. Christ is needed continuously to guard against the reappearance of "the" sin that has been cast out of the soul, just as a candle remains necessary to prevent "darkness"—though the darkness has been dispelled.

E. That God Has a Double Standard

One of the most devastating and harmful misunderstandings surrounding sanctification is that there are two *different* standards within the Christian life—one for the "merely saved" person and another for the believer who goes on to entire sanctification! Such error stymies Christian growth and soothes the conscience of the indifferent and complacent.

1. *Christlikeness the Only Standard*

Those who accept this presupposition often assume that one is not called to absolute and radical commitment to Christ until one comes to the time and point of entire sanctification; that the inner self can go on having its way, while at the same time spiritual life may be indefinitely prolonged. Far too many justify their failure to demonstrate the fruit of the Spirit by the hasty quip that they are not one of the "entirely sanctified," and therefore they are not to be judged by that measure.

There is only one standard for all, namely, Christlikeness. It is just as incumbent upon the regenerated believer to demonstrate the virtues of Christ as it is for the entirely sanctified Christian to do so. There is truth in the oft-quoted statement that "entire sanctification is simply regeneration made easy." The person who is entirely sanctified lives by no higher ideals but has fuller resources of the Spirit to meet the demands of Christian discipleship.

2. *There Is No Half Commitment in the Christian Life*

The life of a Christian, the life of holiness, is a whole piece of cloth. Thus one gives all that he knows of himself to God at his conversion—submits himself to *all* of God's requirements. One does not make a "partial" commitment at regeneration and a "total" commitment at entire sanctification.

In actual practice one prays essentially the same prayer for conversion as one prays for entire sanctification. Technically, we may make valid theological distinctions between a prayer of confession and a prayer of consecration, but the *spirit* and intent of the prayers are identical—namely, *whole commitment* to Christ insofar as one is aware.

In the strictest sense we may say that a person cannot consecrate himself to God until he becomes a child of God, for the simple reason that he has nothing to give but a sinful life. Only a redeemed individual can consecrate.

But one cannot bargain with God. To ask for forgiveness of sins and the alleviation of the condemnation and guilt of sin, while at the same time consciously withholding the self from God, would be the height of presumption. How ludicrous for one to ask for Christ to become his Savior but not his Lord.

One cannot with integrity pray to be converted and deliberately hold back one's talents, one's ambitions, one's plans—until some future, but unknown, time. Such a prayer would accomplish nothing. God requires all there is of us, all that we are capable of giving, at any given moment. Christ will be Lord of *all* our life—however much or little that may be, depending upon our degree of light—or He will not be Lord of *any* of our life.

3. *The Spirit Will Lead the Believer*

Entire sanctification, then, is not optional, but a divine imperative for all who have been made conscious of their need for the purifying of the wellsprings of their life.

As the child of God walks in obedience, he will be made to see by the Spirit a deep propensity to coddle the self, which calls for a radical circumcision and full cleansing of the heart. But having been brought face-to-face with oneself in a new and deeper way, the obedient believer willingly submits to this heart surgery—so that whereas he formerly was "curved in" upon himself (to use Luther's phrase), he now is "curved outwardly" toward God and others. This occurs in the "moment" of entire sanctification.

Some Crucial Questions

All evangelical Christians acknowledge that holiness or sanctification is taught in the Bible, and that it brings believers freedom from sin through the merits of Christ's death. There is wide disagreement, however, regarding the meaning of freedom from sin and when it becomes an actuality in the believer. Dr. Wiley cites four views that are commonly expressed:

a. that holiness is simultaneous with regeneration and completed then

b. that holiness is a matter of spiritual growth from regeneration until physical death

c. that man is made holy in the moment of death

d. that "holiness begins in regeneration, but is completed as an instantaneous work of the Holy Spirit subsequent to regeneration."[6]

The first view we reject because it is contrary to universal Christian experience. Regenerate persons of every age have acknowledged the antagonisms to divine love discovered in them under the illumination of the Holy

Spirit. So strongly have believers been aware of the perverse tendencies of their own natures that many have concluded that there can be no deliverance until death, or perhaps by the means of purgatorial fires.

Dr. Daniel Steele has observed that either these have been mistaken in considering themselves regenerate; or all have backslidden; or they have been in fact regenerated, while struggling with the demands of the sinful self. The first alternatives strain one's credulity, leaving the latter as the only reasonable position. Furthermore, the view that holiness is completed in conversion contradicts the creed of all the orthodox branches of the Church universal.[7]

Christian experience also fails to confirm the views that holiness comes by growth or death. No one claims to have grown into a spiritual state of complete deliverance from the tyranny of a sinful self. Nor are there grounds in the Scriptures for these views.

We believe that holiness is begun in regeneration, is continued by a further instantaneous work of heart cleansing (entire sanctification) wrought by the Holy Spirit subsequent to regeneration, and progresses throughout the life of the believer to glorification. Dr. W. B. Godbey once said: "Entire sanctification is that which we approach gradually, enter *suddenly*, and progress in indefinitely."[8] This position, the Wesleyan position, we believe to be supported by Scripture, reason, and experience.

In every age there have been those who have taught and preached this glorious doctrine. Dr. Vincent Taylor, noted New Testament scholar, has said: "Beyond all doubt the New Testament teaches the absolute necessity of ethical and spiritual perfection."[9] John Wesley described it as an enduement of love that expunges sin.

In fairness we must acknowledge that there is great variety of opinion with regard to *entire* sanctification. With the

Scriptures as our Guide, let us deal as forthrightly as we are able with the leading questions surrounding this teaching.

A. Do the Scriptures Teach a Second Crisis?

When we speak of "crisis," we should be reminded (see Part I, p. 18) that we are not referring to an "emergency" in the life of the believer. Rather, we are asking, Is there a "definite moment" in the Christian walk, following conversion, in which one is purified from all sin? We believe there is!

Defenders of the Wesleyan position have cited numerous scriptures to denote a "secondness" of Christian experience. Not all are equally conclusive. We will note the weaker ones first.

1. *Evidence from Inference*

a. The disciples who were filled with the Holy Spirit on the Day of Pentecost (Acts 2) had been called out "of the world," they had been kept by Christ, they had been obedient to God's Word, and Christ was "glorified" in them (John 17). They had been commissioned by Jesus (Mark 6:7) and were told by Him to "rejoice, because [their] names [were] written in heaven" (Luke 10:20).

b. The account of the Samaritan revival occasioned by the preaching of Philip indicates that the Samaritans had believed, received the Word of God, and were baptized. Subsequently Peter and John were sent from Jerusalem, and they received the Holy Spirit (Acts 8:15-17).

c. Saul of Tarsus was converted on the Damascus road, acknowledged by Ananias' Christian greeting, "Brother," after which Ananias laid his hands on him that he might "be filled with the Holy Spirit" (Acts 9:17, NIV).

d. Cornelius is described as a "devout man," who feared God, gave alms to the people, and "prayed to God alway." To him Peter was sent to lay hands upon him and his household, and "on the Gentiles also was poured out the gift of the Holy Spirit" (Acts 10:45, ASV).

e. The Ephesian disciples had been instructed under the eloquent preaching of Apollos, to whom Aquila and Priscilla "expounded . . . the way of God more perfectly." He, however, went to Corinth. Paul later arrived in Ephesus and asked the disciples, "Have ye received the Holy Spirit since ye believed?" Hearing their negative response, Paul laid his hands on them, and "the Holy Spirit came on them" (Acts 18:24—19:6).

Admittedly the "secondness" inferred from these biblical accounts may be questioned. Frequently it has been pointed out that the persons who knew only the baptism of John had not yet been genuinely converted to Christ in the fullest sense; and, therefore, their reception of the Holy Spirit was their conversion. Or it has been claimed that these cases are unique and illustrate the inauguration of a new age or dispensation.

Although some kind of "secondness" appears to be involved, one would be unwise to build a doctrine on these passages when stronger and more defensible ones are available. "A wise general defends a short line!"

2. *Scriptural Evidence That Is Explicit*

a. Paul's first letter to the Corinthians was addressed "to the church of God in Corinth, to those sanctified in Christ Jesus and called to be holy" (1:2, NIV). The apostle gave thanks that their testimony of Christ had been "confirmed" in them so that they did "not lack any spiritual gift" (vv. 6-7, NIV). Yet he said he must refer to them as "carnal, even as . . . babes in Christ" (3:1 ff.). The climax of the letter came when he showed them the "more excellent way" (12:31 ff.), namely, the way of divine love.

b. John the Baptist seemed to indicate a "secondness" in pointing to Jesus' coming fiery baptism in the

Holy Spirit. "He will throughly purge his floor, and gather his *wheat* into the garner; but he will burn up the *chaff* with unquenchable fire" (Matt. 3:11-12).

H. Orton Wiley has observed that the baptism with the Holy Spirit would effect an internal and spiritual cleansing that would go beyond that of John. The latter was for the remission of sins; the former was for the removal of sin itself. The separation accompanying Christ's baptism with the Spirit is not between the tares and the wheat, which symbolize the wicked and the regenerate, but between the wheat and chaff, or that which belongs to it by nature. First, the wheat is to be garnered for preservation; then the chaff will be consumed by fire.[10]

c. In 2 Cor. 7:1 Paul exhorted the "beloved" to "cleanse [themselves] from all filthiness of the flesh and spirit, perfecting holiness in the fear of God." The meaning is that the initial holiness or cleansing from guilt and "acquired" depravity, that is, depravity resulting from sins committed, is to be perfected at a single stroke by the cleansing from in-being sin.

d. Advocates of the doctrine of entire sanctification frequently note the use of the aorist tense in the Greek, which denotes a momentary, completed act without reference to time, in contrast to the present tense which denotes continuous action.[11] The following examples in passages addressed to believers and referring to their sanctification or cleansing may be cited:

(1) *Rom. 12:1-2.* "I beseech you therefore, brethren, by the mercies of God, that ye present [aorist—a single act not needing to be repeated] your bodies a living sacrifice, holy [indicating their initial sanctification], acceptable [suggesting their justification] unto God" as a condition for being "transformed."[12]

(2) *Rom. 13:14.* "Put ye on [aorist—a single definite

act] the Lord Jesus Christ, and make not provision [that is, quit making provision] for the flesh."

(3) *2 Cor. 1:21-22.* "Now he which stablisheth us with you in Christ, and hath [aorist, as a single, definite act] anointed us, is God; who hath also sealed us [aorist], and given [aorist—gave us a single, definite act] the earnest of the Spirit in our hearts."

(4) *Eph. 1:13.* "In whom also after that ye believed [aorist], ye were sealed [aorist] with that holy Spirit of promise."

(5) *1 Thess. 5:23.* "And the very God of peace sanctify [aorist] you *wholly;* and I pray God your whole spirit and soul and body be preserved blameless unto [in preparation for] the coming of our Lord Jesus Christ."

(6) *Rom. 6:13.* "Yield [aorist—in a specific act of consecration] yourselves unto God, as those that are alive from the dead, and your members as instruments of righteousness unto God." When accompanied by faith, this act of yielding to God the last vestige of self makes possible the full sanctification of our beings by the Holy Spirit.

To be emptied of oneself makes possible the filling of the Holy Spirit. "To be 'filled' with the Spirit does not mean to receive *more* of God, but to give Him *all of ourselves.*"[13]

If one will look with open mind and heart to the Scriptures, particularly to Paul's Epistles, he will find evidence that entire sanctification is a second crisis in Christian experience. We are not sectarian in this. Others outside our circles have found the same thing. For example, Roman Catholic Bishop Fulton J. Sheen, in his sermon "The Psychology of Conversion," has said there is a moral crisis in the soul "when there is an awareness of sin and guilt, . . .

as something inwardly experienced *as a broken relationship"* with God. Then there is a spiritual crisis in

> those who have been seeking perfection but are not yet possessed of the fullness of the Faith. . . . Up to this moment of crisis, they have lived on the surface of their souls. The tension deepens as they realize that, like a plant, they have roots which need greater spiritual depths and branches meant for communion with the heavens above. The growing sense of dissatisfaction with their own ordinariness is accompanied by a passionate craving for surrender, sacrifice, and abandonment to God's Holy Will. . . . They have the desire; they need only the courage with which to pass through the crisis in which, through . . . surrender, they will find themselves victors in the captivity of Divinity.[14]

Could a clearer statement be found among the staunchest holiness advocates?

3. *Substance Takes Precedence over Circumstance*

The question is often raised as to whether one who has been entirely sanctified and later goes back to a life of sin must again go through separate stages of new birth and entire sanctification. In logic these are distinct steps, and normally they are separated by some interval of time. But in actual practice there need be no appreciable span of time. The stages are simply levels of awareness of need, and where the need is known and conditions are met, God's grace is sufficient. John Fletcher observed that though "sanctification is not generally the work of a day nor of a year," God can "cut short his work in righteousness."[15]

In answering the question affirmatively, Is entire sanctification a second crisis? we have cited the biblical evidence, which is confirmed by normal Christian experience. However, we would be wise to observe Wesley's distinction between the "substance" and the "circumstance" of this teaching.

The former has to do with the truth itself; the latter, with the way the truth becomes reality to the believer. "[We] are all agreed," he wrote, "we may be saved from all sin before death. The substance then is settled."[16] How God brings it about is secondary.

The more important question is: Have I yielded up myself to God to be controlled by Him? Have I relinquished my self-sovereignty and been cleansed and filled by the abiding presence of the Holy Spirit?

> *Refining Fire, go thro' my heart;*
> *Illuminate my soul;*
> *Scatter Thy life thro' ev'ry part,*
> *And sanctify the whole.*
> —CHARLES WESLEY

B. Can Depravity or Self-centeredness Be Done Away?

We must keep in mind that "original sin," sometimes called *"inherited* depravity," is not a substance or physical entity. It is a spirit of selfishness, of anarchy or rebellion against God. Paul refers to it as *"the* sin" (Rom. 5—8).

1. *Original Sin Is like Organized Selfishness*

This "in-being sin" is something like a "complex"— that is, "the instincts organized into a system to give a set reaction to objects or experiences presented by the environment. It is disliked by the dominant portion of the personality and is therefore repressed . . . as much as possible." Under the influence of in-being sin "the instinctive life is organized to forward self-will in opposition to the sovereignty of God and the Lordship of Christ" (see Rom. 8:7).

In an unregenerate person, only occasionally does the true self—spurred by conscience—attempt to resist the influence of in-being sin. When regeneration occurs, the Spirit of God quickens man's spirit, and the will seeks to bring the whole personality into submission to God. But the will is confronted with this complex—this "selfish" system—which controls the instinctive life. This system may be suppressed by the regenerated will, but in times of temptation it may rise in rebellion. The result is an inward conflict—self divided against itself.

In entire sanctification this "selfish" system (complex) is broken up and the conflict resolved. The instinctive life must still be disciplined, but this can be done without organized resistance from within.[17]

2. *The New Testament Words*

It is significant to observe that while the Greek language had many words that mean *suppression*—"hold down," "control," "close," "strangle," "choke," "subdue," and so on—none is used in the New Testament with reference to sin. Rather, the biblical writers used strong and decisive words like "purge," "purify," "remove dross," "eliminate," "annul," "abolish," "put an end to," "dissolve," "melt," "crucify," "break up," "put off," "mortify," "kill," "render extinct" (see Part I, p. 25).

3. *The Death of Sin*

In his letter to the Romans the apostle Paul wrote: "Knowing this, that our old man is crucified [lit., "was crucified"] with him, that the body of sin might be destroyed, that henceforth we should not serve sin" (6:6). Crucifixion in the light of Roman custom could mean but one thing—death. Upon the cross of shame our old man of sin was crucified in company with Christ. This *provisional* death is made reality in our life through faith. By faith we die with Christ, whose death becomes our death, setting us free from sin's tyranny. We become "dead indeed unto sin" (v. 11).

The writer of the Colossian letter leaves little room for misunderstanding: "In whom also ye are circumcised with the circumcision made without hands, in putting off the body of the sins of the flesh by the circumcision of Christ" (2:11). Can anything other than the destruction of sin be intended? The rite of circumcision had but one implication— separation and mortification. This circumcision of the heart, this removal of the body of the sins of the flesh, is accomplished "without hands," that is, by a supernatural act of God.

Yes! The Scriptures teach that through God's mighty act in Christ a deathblow to depravity or self-centeredness is dealt. How irreverent it would be to place limitations on the nature or power of God!

C. What About Remaining Humanity? the Self?

It is often said that when one receives a holy heart, the self is destroyed. Yet sound psychological insights have made us aware of the importance and necessity of selfhood. To destroy the self would be to destroy the person himself, for, like the will, it is essential to human individuality.

1. *Crucifixion of the Sinful Self*

The terminology is unfortunate, but the point it is attempting to make is sound and scriptural. The self that is sinful and self-sufficient, that seeks to find acceptance with God by self-effort, the self that wants to serve God but in its own way and time—that is the self that must be destroyed and to which Paul referred when he said: "I am crucified with Christ" (Gal. 2:20). This selfish, sinful self must be cleansed and renovated and purged by the baptism with the Holy Spirit.

Unfortunately, sin blinds persons to their need for the crucifixion of this sinful self. Only when this occurs and divine love fills the heart can one love God "supremely," others "sacrificially," and oneself "unselfishly."

2. Development of the True Self

Kierkegaard, 19th-century Danish philosopher, once remarked: "No man needs to be told when he has lost a wife, a limb, or a fortune; but how few men seem to notice the loss of the [true] self."

Entire sanctification is not the destruction of the self properly understood, but the uncovering, the liberating, and the empowering of the true self by the Holy Spirit. The life of holiness is the continuing development of this self in accordance with God's desire and will.

While one's will has been captured, it has not been "broken." One lives as a willing servant, captivated by a Master who rules by love. The true self in proper relation to God does not live in bondage, with the fear of a servant. Rather, he delights in the law of the Lord, which is written on his heart (Ps. 1:2; Jer. 31:33).

The story is told of a king who wanted to do something to honor one of his subjects. He promised him his daughter in marriage, a home in the palace, meals at the king's table. But the subject rejected the overture, saying he would feel uncomfortable in the presence of the king.

When the self finds itself in God, it is no longer uncomfortable before Him. Where the heart is made holy, there emerges the real self, which enjoys His holy presence. "Herein is our love made perfect, that we may have boldness in the day of judgment" (1 John 4:17).

3. Discipline of the Human Self

The entirely sanctified believer will continue to have basic instincts and urges that are a part of his or her humanness. These are clearly related to the sentiments of life, such as love and hate, acquisitiveness and pride, pity and patriotism. These impulses have been perverted by sin. "Hunger is not sin, but gluttony and intemperance are. Sex [within the divine limits] is not sin, but unchastity and adultery are.

The desire to possess something is not sin, but covetousness, theft, and dishonesty are. Combativeness is not sin, but assault and murder are. Self-regard, even self-love, is not sin, but vanity and luxurious self-display are."[18] Temptation is not sin—yielding to that which God prohibits is.

When do the human instincts become sinful? Not until one's *will* makes it his own. If one harbors the temptation, gluts his imagination, feeds upon and enjoys the thought of evil—then it will become sin, an evil thought. Wherever the will is captured, it is sin—even though the desire does not issue in a misdeed. This is Jesus' meaning in teaching that one can be guilty of murder or adultery when he is controlled by hatred or unbridled desire (Matt. 5:21-22, 27-28). But if one refuses to yield his will, the impulse bids unsuccessfully for moral stature.

Does the disciplining of the instincts involve an inner struggle? In one sense, any temptation involves an inward test because there is appeal to the mind through the senses. But there is no necessary discord regarding one's fundamental loyalty and allegiance. All organized resistance has ceased. The whole self has been given to God to direct.[19]

The body must be disciplined by the enabling presence of the Spirit. "The fruit of the Spirit is . . . self-control" (Gal. 5:22-23, NIV). There is a "suppression," properly understood, within the life of the Christian. Paul expressed it pointedly: "I beat my body and make it my slave so that after I have preached to others, I myself will not be disqualified for the prize" (1 Cor. 9:27, NIV).

"There is a *sinful* self to be crucified with Christ; a *true* self to be realized in Christ; and a *human* self to be disciplined by Christ" (attributed to J. O. McClurkan).

D. Does Failure Ever Occur in the Entirely Sanctified?

Yes! Many live frustrated and defeated lives because they have thought failures are inconsistent with being entirely sanctified. Others have covered over their failures by easing their conscience to the point that they almost live in deceit and hypocrisy.

1. *Failure Needs Forgiveness Too*

Because man's body has been affected by the Fall, on occasion he will "think, speak, or act wrong; not indeed through a defect of love, but through a defect of knowledge."[20] The accuracy of this observation of John Wesley is confirmed by experience. Through some spoken word, some missed opportunity to serve another, the best of Christ's followers on occasion fail.

For these failures we need the atonement of Christ and should seek forgiveness. If we have injured others, we must go and make amends as Jesus taught us to do (Matt. 5:23-24). We should not preface our remarks with "If I have hurt you . . ." Rather, we should openly acknowledge our failure and ask forgiveness.

2. *A Mark of Christian Maturity*

Wesley wrote: "If you have at any time thought, spoke, or acted wrong, be not backward to acknowledge it. Never dream that [confession] will hurt the cause of God; no, it will further it. Be therefore open and frank . . . do not seek either to evade or disguise [your failure]; but let it appear just as it is, and you will thereby not hinder, but adorn, the gospel."[21]

One who is following close to Christ, progressing in Christlikeness, will acknowledge, confess, and identify his failure, while overlooking the faults of others (James 5:16). *One's spiritual maturity may be measured by the length of time he allows to elapse between his consciousness of failure and his taking these steps!*[22] He will trust the Lord for forgiveness and cleansing and will continue in obedience and uninterrupted fellowship with God.

The life of holiness at every stage is a "moment by moment" life. The entirely sanctified man knows he has been lifted to a new level of spiritual living (see Rom. 8:2, 9; Gal. 2:20). He need not fall—nor should he plan even to fail—but should a lapse occur, he has "one who speaks to the Father in [his] defense—Jesus Christ, the Righteous One. He is the atoning sacrifice for [his] sins" (1 John 2:1-2, NIV). The continual aim of his life will be the glory of God, and he will be empowered to "press toward the mark for the prize of the high calling of God in Christ Jesus" (Phil. 3:14).

CONCLUSION

We have looked at some common misunderstandings and crucial questions regarding entire sanctification and the life of holiness. But the most basic question of all is, Which direction am I traveling spiritually? Am I being obedient to all the light I have? Is my all in this moment fully given to Christ? Is there inner assurance of full acceptance with God? Is my life bearing the fruit of the Spirit?

Or am I defending and protecting myself against God? withholding myself from Him?

Cleansing, purity, power for life and service, fellowship, and love for God and others come only on condition of penitence, full consecration, and trusting faith. Let us commit our all to Christ and pray:

> *Have Thine own way, Lord! Have Thine own way!*
> *Hold o'er my being absolute sway!*
> *Fill with Thy Spirit till all shall see*
> *Christ only, always living in me!*
> —ADELAIDE A. POLLARD

8

The Adventure of Holy Living

"Real holiness has love for its essence, humility for its clothing, the good of others as its employment, and the honor of God as its end" (Emmons).

A new covenant! Restoration in the divine image! These two themes run like threads through all the Bible to describe man's relationship with God as it should be and as it can be! The apostle Paul beautifully wove these together in 2 Cor. 3. He showed the superiority of the new covenant over the old covenant given to Moses at Sinai.

As the mediator of the old covenant, Moses was granted direct communion with the Lord, so radiant that he was compelled to veil his countenance in order to hide God's glory. However, that experience was temporary and available only to a choice group of Old Testament worthies.

Now in Christ there is a better covenant; Christ is the new Mediator, and transformation into His image is universally possible for all. Thus Paul said: "But we all, with open face [that is, no veils on our faces] beholding as in a glass [reflecting like a mirror] the glory of the Lord, are changed into the same image from glory to glory, even as by the Spirit of the Lord" (v. 18).

1. *There Is No Spiritual Elite*

This direct communion with Christ and continuing transformation into His likeness is for all God's children. All of us! The *Revised Standard Version* renders verse 18 thus: "We all, with unveiled face, beholding the glory of the Lord *are being changed [metamorphoumetha]* into his likeness from one degree of glory to another."

Paul expressed the same thought in his admonition to the Roman believers: "Be ye transformed [*metamorphousthe,* present continuous tense] by the renewing of your mind" (12:2). A form of the same word *(metemorphōthē)* also is used to describe our Lord's transfiguration, when His countenance "did shine as the sun" (Matt. 17:2; Mark 9:2).

God's plan is that His children continuously will be changed (metamorphosed) into the likeness of Christ. In the New Testament every Christian is a holy person who reflects the radiance of his Lord. Holy living characterizes all believers and not merely a spiritually elite within the Church. God's design for a holy people is not a call to supersaints, but a gift to all trusting disciples.

2. *The Scope of God's Grace*

We have seen that God effects His holiness in man progressively or in successive stages. H. Orton Wiley, dean of Nazarene theologians, observed: "Each of these stages is marked by a *gradual* approach and an *instantaneous* consummation in experience, and the stages together mark the *full* scope of sanctifying grace. Thus 'in His administration of sanctifying grace the Holy Spirit proceeds by degrees.'"[1]

John Wesley acknowledged these stages in the life of the believer by distinguishing the "natural" man, "awakened" man, and "evangelical" man. The unawakened sinner has "neither fear nor love"; the convicted sinner has "fear, but no love"; the converted man has "both fear and love"; and the entirely sanctified man has "love without fear."[2]

Because sanctification and holiness run all the way through the Christian life, and because there are also distinct and identifiable moments of commitment and faith, namely, conversion and entire sanctification, it is often said that sanctification is both a *crisis* and a *process*. Bishop Moule has stated it well: "It is a crisis with a view of a process."

To be converted to Christ is to be set on the road to moral and spiritual perfection, to a life of holiness. Within this life process, there is a decisive moment possible that brings the believer complete deliverance from all sin and entire devotement to the will of God. This crisis we know as "entire sanctification."

Conversion removes man's guilt by forgiveness; it overcomes man's alienation through acceptance and adoption into God's family; it destroys man's death with life and new birth (regeneration). Entire sanctification cleanses man's fundamental pollution of sin—sin in embryo, the being of sin, the fountain and condition of sin—and effects coherence and integrity of the self. (See Part I, p. 19.)

In this closing chapter, we will look at several minimal and elemental affirmations that should illuminate our understanding of entire sanctification and enhance our adventure in holy living.[3]

THE ESSENCE OF ENTIRE SANCTIFICATION IS CHRISTLIKE LOVE

There are many ways to describe entire sanctification. The psychologist speaks of it as "love"; the prophet as "righteousness"; the priest as "holiness"; the philosopher as "perfection." Each of these terms has biblical support. However, the personal term "love" seems more adequate, with the other terms serving as modifiers. Thus perhaps we should speak of the righteousness of love, the holiness of love, the perfection of love.

The love exhibited by the sanctified person is not a mere emotion or sentiment; it is the active willing of the well-being of others. It is God's kind of love *(agapē)* "poured out . . . into our hearts" (Rom. 5:5, NIV), "producing love to all mankind . . . ; expelling the love of the world, the love of [sinful] pleasure, of ease, of honour, of money, together with pride, anger, self-will, and every other evil temper; in a word, changing the 'earthly, sensual, devilish' mind into the 'mind which was in Christ Jesus.'" Entire sanctification is "love excluding sin; love filling the heart, taking up the whole capacity of the soul."[4]

A. The Perfection of Love

Entire sanctification sometimes goes by the term "Christian perfection." There is much misunderstanding concerning "perfection." But it is a biblical word. Paul stated that the aim of his apostleship was to "present every man *perfect* in Christ Jesus" (Col. 1:28). He indicated that he had found one kind of perfection—*realized* perfection, while yet reaching for another—*resurrection* perfection (Phil. 3:15, 12). In the Sermon on the Mount, Jesus commanded His followers to be "perfect," as their Heavenly Father is perfect (Matt. 5:48).

The word "perfect" is used approximately 138 times in the Scripture, including about 50 times with reference to human character. It means to perform, to execute fully, to bring to reality, or to carry into practice. The Greek word for "perfect" *(teleios)* suggests the idea of attaining to an end or goal. A thing is said to be perfect if it is functioning as it was designed to function.

The end or perfection God has in mind for man is holiness, a perfection in love. We are not commanded by Jesus to be *as* perfect in love *as* our Heavenly Father, but to be perfect in love *like* our Heavenly Father. Entire sanctification or Christian perfection is, as Wesley put it, "the loving God with all our heart, mind, soul, and strength."

He continued, "This implies, that no wrong temper, none contrary to love, remains in the soul; and that all the thoughts, words, and actions, are governed by pure love."[5] Every desire is in subjection to the obedience of Christ. The will is entirely subject to the will of God, and the affections are wholly fixed on Him.

Christian perfection is not perfection in knowledge or freedom from ignorance, mistakes, and poor judgment. While it is freedom from evil thoughts (in which one feeds the imagination and relishes the thought), it is not freedom from passing thoughts *about* evil. Nor is it freedom from temptation or the effects of infirmities.

In entire sanctification, the human, normal desires and emotions are not removed, but they are redirected and purified. One is made clean in desire and clean or undivided in his devotions, affections, and loyalties. He is enabled to "possess [his] vessel," that is, control his body (1 Thess. 4:4). He is not freed *from* temptation, but made conqueror in the midst of it.

Because of what entire sanctification is not, Wesley referred to it as "Christian perfection," rather than "sinless" perfection. Paul made it clear that God has not called us for the purpose of uncleanness, but for the purpose of sanctification or cleanness (1 Thess. 4:7).

B. Being and Becoming

The Greek term for "perfect" has another meaning. It suggests completeness, full stature, or maturity. The perfection in love accomplished instantaneously in a moment is yet a progressively growing love. Thus in 1 Thessalonians Paul exhorted the believers to "abound more and more" in love (4:1, 10).

He conveyed the idea of "completeness" (though the word itself is different) with his comment: "Night and day praying exceedingly that we might see your face, and might *perfect* that which is lacking in your faith" (3:10). Paul desired to "round out to completeness" (Williams) the "defects" or shortcomings of their faith (Alford). The word employed here *(katartisai)* was sometimes used to describe the mending of nets, suggesting a life of discipline or training for service.

The Christian is to be growing continuously, allowing the Lord to mend him or mold him so as to make him effective as an instrument in His hand.

> *I'm a person God is making,*
> *Like a statue God is shaping;*
> *God is changing me, correcting;*
> *God's intent on my perfecting!*

Christian perfection is not a finished character. It is a commitment to "becoming" what God wants to make of us.

C. Perfection Is a Spirit

To be perfect is to possess the mind of Christ who "made himself of *no reputation*," took "the form of a *servant*," and "became *obedient* unto death, even the death of the cross" (Phil. 2:5-8). "The fruits of the Spirit [in us] are the virtues of Christ."

Jesus illustrates the meaning of perfection in Matt. 5. It is to go "the second mile" as a means of serving another; it is to give one's cloak after his coat has been already taken; it is to pray for one's enemies; it is to turn the other cheek. To the Jew the "right cheek" symbolized his personal pride or ego, and one of the greatest insults was to hit a Jew with the back of the hand on the cheek. In requiring His disciples to turn the other cheek, Jesus was saying that they were not to retaliate out of a sense of injured pride or ego. This is perfection!

Simply stated, Christian perfection is Christlikeness, the spirit of Jesus portrayed when He was being nailed to the Cross: "Father, forgive them; for they know not what they do" (Luke 23:34). It is the spirit of Stephen, who prayed as he was being stoned: "Lord, lay not this sin to their charge" (Acts 7:60).

For this reason Wesley said wisely that if in seeking Christian perfection we are looking for anything else than love, which freely pours itself out in sacrificial and forgiving service, we are looking "wide of the mark."

> *Come in, come in, Thou Heavenly Guest!*
> *Nor hence again remove;*
> *But sup with me and let the feast*
> *Be everlasting love.*
> —CHARLES WESLEY

ALL CONSCIOUS SIN—INWARD AND OUTWARD— IS BANISHED IN ENTIRE SANCTIFICATION

No sin in the life can be tolerated by the true Christian. It matters not whether one is a new believer or a seasoned disciple, there must be no sin as understood in its primary biblical meaning. Salvation means "deliverance" from sin.

It is frequently stated that in justification we are delivered from the *past* or guilt of sin; simultaneously in regeneration we are delivered from the *power* of sin; in entire sanctification we are delivered from the *pollution* of sin; and in glorification we shall be delivered from the *presence* and effects of sin. But at every stage of the Christian or holy life we are being delivered or saved continuously moment by moment. (See Part I, p. 20.)

A. The Sovereignty of Grace

For Wesley, Christian perfection or entire sanctification is another way of describing and celebrating the "sovereignty of grace." He spoke of the stages of the Christian life by using the language of John (1 John 2:13-14): "little children" (babes in Christ), "young men" (those who have begun to be established and assured), and "fathers" (those made perfect in love).

However, even babes in Christ do not commit sin. The power and dominion of sin, and of sinning, is broken. All believers are "made free from outward sin." "Whosoever is born of God sinneth not; but he that is begotten of God keepeth himself, and that wicked one toucheth him not" (1 John 5:18). He does not sin "wilfully" or "habitually." Every true Christian "is so far perfect as not to commit sin."

A new Christian normally experiences such a change that he will "imagine that all sin is gone; that it is utterly rooted out of [the] heart." He infers, says Wesley: "I *feel* no sin; therefore, I *have* none: It does not *stir;* therefore, it does not *exist:* It has no *motion;* therefore, it has no *being!*" But until one is sanctified *wholly,* sin is "only suspended, not destroyed."[6]

B. Crucified with Christ

Entire sanctification is full salvation—deliverance from the pollution or in-being of sin—from pride, self-will, anger. The Christian will have no doubt of the favor of God, but he will come to a "conviction," wrought by the Holy Spirit, "of the *sin* which still *remains* in [the] heart; of . . . *the carnal mind,* which 'does still *remain* . . . even in them that are regenerate;' although it does no longer *reign.*"

In time the believer discerns a spirit of selfishness or unchristlikeness—"so that we are now more ashamed of our best duties than formerly of our worst sins." We confess our absolute "helplessness, . . . our utter inability to think one good thought, or to form one good desire;. and much more, to speak one word aright, or to perform one good action, but through [Christ's] free almighty grace."[7]

Paul's phrase, "crucified with Christ" (Gal. 2:20), describes a deliverance from *inward* as well as *outward* sin.

One who is sanctified wholly is "dead indeed unto sin," to all carnally selfish desires, and to everything that is contrary to God's will. But he is "alive unto God," demonstrated by love to God and loving-kindness to one's fellows (Rom. 6:11). Not only does one enjoy cleansing or freedom from sinning and from original sin, but also his will is brought into complete devotement to the will of God.

God does not *break* man's will. Rather, he captures or *draws* man's will by love. The entirely sanctified are preserved in love (1 Thess. 3:12; 4:9-10). There is a difference between fear and love. Fear says, "Must I?" Love says, "May I?" God puts His law in our love—we become "inlawed," so that we delight in His will. It is because of God's activity *in* us that Augustine could make the bold challenge: "Love God and do as you please." He knew that the person who is sanctified wholly will do right as surely as water runs downhill.

C. Offering Up of the Whole Self

All who are sanctified offer themselves and their service as a living sacrifice or offering to God (Rom. 12:1). They do not seek to please men so as to win their applause if some Christian principle must be compromised. It is God they seek to satisfy, not men (1 Thess. 4:1). The commandment of the Lord is "Walk before me"—not before the world or even pharisaical religionists—"and be perfect" (Gen. 17:1). Those who are wholly Christ's seek to live a "blameless" life. They know it will not be "faultless" (1 Thess. 3:13).

Fundamentally, blame is appropriate only where the motive is wrong. Actions that are less than they should be, but which are done with high and pure intentions, are faulty—but not sinful—and arise out of man's infirmities of body and mind. "Blamelessness" is possible now to the

Christian, and at the last day Christ will "present us *fault-less* before the presence of his glory with exceeding joy" (Jude 24).

Aware of his faulty actions, the truly sanctified person will not seek to justify them but will fully depend upon the continuous cleansing of Christ's blood. He is not self-defensive but is sensitive to the leadings and checks of the Spirit. As he acknowledges his errors, the blood of Christ continues to cleanse from all sin and to preserve personal fellowship with God (1 John 1:7).

The holy life is one of continuous penitence and reliance upon God. We need atonement for our infirmities and errors. To say the entirely cleansed heart does not need Christ's atonement would be like saying that because it is noon, we do not need the sun. It is the sun that brings the noonday light; and it is Christ who gives us moment-by-moment freedom from sin.

D. Common Objections to Christian Perfection

To be entirely sanctified does not mean that one is "not able to sin." It is to be enabled "not to sin." "If we will we may; if we won't we can't." Some have supposed that sin is desirable in order to make man humble. John Fletcher, Wesley's trusted associate, illustrated the absurdity of this reasoning:

Who has more sin than Satan? And who is prouder? Did sin make our first parents humble? If it did not, why do our brethren suppose that its nature is altered for the better? Who was humbler than Christ? But was he indebted to sin for his humility? Do we not see daily that the more sinful men are, the prouder they are also?[8]

Critics of the doctrine of Christian perfection have raised numerous objections: the doctrine of perfection leads to pride; it exalts believers to the state of the Pharisees; it fills with conceit and a "holier than thou" attitude; it sets repentance aside; it makes one slight Christ and trust himself; it makes unnecessary the discipline of the body; it makes the prayer "Forgive us our sins" superfluous.

To these objections we observe that the growing Christian has a keen awareness of his involuntary trespasses and always seeks forgiveness. Fletcher, whom Wesley described as the most saintly man of the 18th century and possibly since the apostle Paul, often set down his deepest thoughts and confessions in correspondence to friends.

To Charles Wesley he wrote regularly. He would request, "O Charles, please pray for me, that I will be filled with the Holy Spirit." Shortly after, he would write, but with joy: "O Charles, rejoice with me. The Comforter has come in His fulness." Soon he would write again: "O Charles, please pray with me that I will be filled with the Holy Spirit. The Lord is showing me daily areas of my life which need improvement." Then later: "O Charles, rejoice with me. I have been filled with the fulness of God."

Were his requests to be "filled with the Holy Spirit" indications that he was not entirely sanctified? Indeed not! They were just the opposite. As the Spirit guided Fletcher and gave him new light, he walked in that light. He was growing and expanding spiritually. Thus he prayed for new and fresh fillings of the Spirit. His experience fits Paul's admonition: "Be filled [present continuous tense] with the Spirit," or literally, "Keep on being filled with the Spirit" (Eph. 5:18).

The Holy Spirit, who is given to the believer in conversion, reveals man's need for complete cleansing of the heart and for the fullness of the Spirit. He shows one's "lack" (1 Thess. 3:10) and reveals the possibility of entire sanctification (John 16:8-13; 17:17). It is the Holy Spirit who creates a hunger and thirst for this unfathomable relationship with God. And Christ's promise is: "Blessed are they which do hunger and thirst after righteousness: for they shall be *filled*" (Matt. 5:6).

ENTIRE SANCTIFICATION COMES BY FAITH AND IN AN INSTANT

At his Damascus road conversion, Paul was commissioned to go to the Gentiles "to open their eyes, and to turn them from darkness to light, and from the power of Satan unto God, that they may receive forgiveness of sins, and inheritance among them which are *sanctified by faith* that is in me" (Acts 26:18).

However one may interpret the Cornelius incident recorded in Acts 10, it is significant that Peter, in recounting the experience years later at the Council of Jerusalem, said: "God . . . put no difference between us [the disciples at Pentecost] and them [the house of Cornelius], purifying their hearts by faith" (Acts 15:8-9).

Whatever else may be asserted of entire sanctification, it is a divine work and not a human one. It is not attained by self-denigration aimed at total resignation. No aspect of salvation is by "works, lest any man should boast" (Eph. 2:9).

> *And every virtue we possess,*
> *And every victory won,*
> *And every thought of holiness*
> *Are His alone.*
> —HARRIET AUBER

A. Faith Involves Obedience and Consecration

Faith is the only condition to be met, although it is the faith of full commitment. Complete consecration of oneself, one's substance, and one's service makes possible the personal, appropriating faith that brings one into entire sanctification. That faith, which lays hold of the promise that the "altar [Christ] sanctifies the gift" (Matt. 23:19), grows out of a complete renunciation of everything known to be opposed to the will of God for us. It is an irrevocable and consummate consecration to God, a death to one's selfish desires.

The faith that brings the blessing is a conviction that God has promised sanctification in the Scriptures, that He will perform His word, that He will do it *now*, and that He does it. But one act of faith is insufficient. One's faith must be his life. As one cannot live on indefinitely by one breath, so one cannot sustain spiritual life by a single moment of faith.

This is consistent with the repeated teaching of the New Testament in which the word "believe" is always in the progressive present, indicating a continuing responsibility on the part of the believer to maintain the new "walk of faith," which includes obedience and love (cf. John 1:7; 3:16-17; 20:3; Acts 13:39; Rom. 10:10). There is no state of grace that does not presuppose dependence upon Christ and therefore continuing faith in Christ.

B. Faith Can Be Exercised in a Moment

Since entire sanctification is by faith, it is wrought *instantaneously.*[9] "Certainly you may look for it *now,* if you believe it is by faith," wrote Wesley. Works require time— the idea that you must *do* something or *be* something. To deny that it comes by faith, therefore, is a form of pride, self-righteousness. To claim that one is not yet good enough is a subtle form of self-reliance.

But, said Wesley, "If you seek it by faith, you may expect it as you are, and if as you are, then expect it now." There is "an inseparable connection between these points —expect it *by faith;* expect it *as you are;* and expect it *now!* To deny one of them is to deny them all."[10]

Someone has said: "No man is sanctified until he believes. Every man, when he believes, is sanctified." This truth prompted J. W. Alexander to exult: "There cannot be named a pursuit or enterprise of human beings, in which there is so little possibility of failure, as praying for sanctification."

ENTIRE SANCTIFICATION CARRIES
ITS OWN ASSURANCE

The Bible teaches not only that man can be made holy, delivered from sin, but also that he may be inwardly conscious or assured that this is so. This doctrine of the witness of the Spirit grows out of the character of God himself, who created man in His own image so that He might communicate with him. A part of the image includes man's God-given ability to respond to God, to know God, and to be known of Him. The witness of the Spirit is not some esoteric, emotional, or mystical experience. It is the communication of God to man that he is "accepted in the beloved" (Eph. 1:6).

There are two verses that are almost always referred to in any discussion of the witness of the Spirit:

Rom. 8:16. "The Spirit himself testifies with our spirit that we are God's children" (NIV).

Heb. 10:14-16. "For by a single offering he has perfected for all time those who are sanctified. And the Holy Spirit also bears witness to us; for after saying,

'This is the covenant that I will make with them
after those days, says the Lord:
I will put my laws on their hearts,
and write them on their minds,'
then he adds,
'I will remember their sins and their misdeeds no
more'" (RSV).

Other scriptures related to the Spirit's witness include

1 Cor. 2:12; Gal. 4:6; 1 John 3:24; 4:13; 5:6. While each may stand by itself, it is well to remember that Christian assurance is a gift of God, arising out of His mercy and lovingkindness.

A. The Objective and Subjective Witness (See Part I, pp. 26-27.)

The witness of the Spirit provides a personal quality that makes the Christian life one of joy, satisfaction, peace, stability, contentment, endurance. The twin doctrines of the witness of the Spirit and of entire sanctification are distinctive in Wesleyan teaching and preaching.

How do we know we have been cleaned of "in-being" sin? Wesley's answer is biblical: "By the witness and the fruit of the Spirit." He spoke of the "objective" witness, which is simply God's Word and promise. For example, God has promised to "circumcise thine heart, and the heart of thy seed, to love the LORD thy God with all thine heart, and with all thy soul" (Deut. 30:6).

The witness of the Spirit that one is sanctified wholly is a "divine evidence and conviction that what God hath promised, he is able to perform," and that "he is able and willing to do it now," and a "divine evidence and conviction that he doeth it. In that hour it is done."

Then there is the "subjective" witness of the Spirit. This includes the *direct* witness of God's Spirit with mine that I am accepted of God. That is, there is no condemnation, but comfort and pleasure in the presence of God. The other part of this subjective or inner testimony is the *indirect* witness to the human spirit. In a sense it is an "inference" arising out of the fact that one has a "good conscience," which avoids offending either God or man (Acts 24:16).

In other words, from the "fruit of the Spirit" manifest in one's life—"love, joy, peace, longsuffering, gentleness, goodness, faith, meekness, temperance" (Gal. 5:22-23)—one is assured of God's activity in him. The fruit must be present, otherwise the inference is mere illusion.[11]

To substitute for this inner witness with some external sign or physical phenomenon is to go beyond the teaching of the Scriptures. The obvious danger and error in doing so is to shift the primary emphasis from the Spirit himself to the validating expression. To set up some particular gift as "the" evidence of being sanctified wholly, or of being baptized or filled with the Spirit, exalts the gift rather than the Giver.

B. The Basis for Christian Assurance

Scripture has much to say about evidences and Christian assurance. John spoke six times of *knowing* that we are abiding in Christ, are of the truth, and have passed from death to life (see 1 John 2:3, 5, 29; 3:14, 24; 4:13).

Peter said that the Christian has been given a *"lively hope"* and the *witness of the Spirit* (see Acts 15:8-9; 1 Pet. 1:3-4). Paul affirmed that we have been *sealed* and have *much assurance* (2 Cor. 1:21-22; 5:1; Gal. 4:6; Eph. 4:30; 1 Thess. 1:5). The writer of Hebrews stated that we have *confidence* (10:35).

The Bible positively teaches *that* we can know that we are accepted of God. *How* we know is just as positively stated as is the fact of our knowledge. John is unequivocal in asserting that we know we have passed from death to life "because we love the brethren" (1 John 3:14); we know we know God because "we keep his commandments" (2:3); we know we are "in him" because the "love of God [is] perfected" in us (2:5); we know our love has been made perfect because we feel comfortable in the presence of a holy God (4:16-19). And Paul relied upon the personal witness of the Holy Spirit (2 Cor. 1:21-22; Gal. 4:6; Eph. 1:13), including the fruit of the Spirit (Gal. 5:22-23).

Christian assurance is not information *about* God or mere acquaintance with teachings concerning Him. It arises out of personal "knowledge," involving an intimate, vital relationship with Him. Christian assurance always finds its source here, enabling one to trust and affirm: "I *know* whom I have believed, and am persuaded that he is able to keep that which I have committed unto him" (2 Tim. 1:12).

Total certainty is possible but issues only from total commitment and complete cleansing.

ENTIRE SANCTIFICATION IS GIVEN IN THIS LIFE —NOT FOR THE MONASTERY

The promises of the new covenant inscribed on man's heart, and of the restoration of man in the divine image, have no meaning unless their fulfillment is planned for this life. The good news is that these can become reality now. In entire sanctification the benefits of these promises are enjoyed.

Sin alienates from God. Holiness or holy living is required to see God. If these biblical teachings are taken seriously, then to deny Christian perfection or entire sanctification is to affirm some form of "purgatory" (i.e., death itself or following death) or to accept the alternative that sinful man will be banished from God's presence forever.

Entire sanctification obviously is designed for man's life now because of what it does for him. Some of these benefits Paul outlined in 1 Thessalonians. In the early part of the letter he spoke of the total life of holiness begun in regeneration, and then he proceeded to speak of a moment of absolute commitment and cleansing to which the believer will be led (chap. 7). It is this relationship to God—entire sanctification—that makes possible the *continuing* life of holiness that Paul discussed in the beginning chapters.

A. Wholeness and Balance

The passage suggests that entire sanctification brings "wholeness" and "completeness"—*beauty!* The discord of man's selfish nature is removed, and harmony with God's will is secured. Paul prayed that these believers would be sanctified "wholly," or "through and through" (Luther). He underscored the truth that the means of receiving this "wholeness" is "the God of peace" (5:23). Entire sanctification brings peace and poise not otherwise possible.

This inner rest makes something beautiful of one's life. The materials of the Temple were originally in a rough state. But put into the hands of cunning workmen, they were brought up into useful and beautiful forms. Likewise, in the hands of the God of peace, the "great Artificer," the believer is molded into something useful and beautiful.

Wholeness includes not only beauty but *balance* as well. Paul spoke of the sanctification and cleansing of our "whole spirit and soul and body" (5:23). In entire sanctification these are integrated and related so as to work together for the glory of God. The integrity of the self is fully realized. No power in the universe is able to destroy this wholeness!

B. Service and Stability

Both cleansing and dedication are a part of biblical sanctification. As in the Old Testament the vessels had to be cleansed before they could be used in divine worship, so we too must be cleansed before we are fit for the Master's use. This cleansing and separation is accomplished in entire sanctification.

However, separation is not withdrawal from life or into a monastery. Jesus prayed for His disciples that they might be sanctified, equipped to be "sent into the world," even as the Father had sent Him into the world (John

17:15-18). There will be separation from the spirit of the world—its covetousness, restlessness, conversation, conduct, and selfishness. But there will be love, compassion, active seeking to serve others in every relationship of life.

To be holy is to care for the hungry, the thirsty, the stranger, the naked, the sick, and the imprisoned, as Jesus taught (Matt. 25:35-40). Goethe, the great German writer, said: "Behavior is a mirror in which everyone displays his image." Those who bear the divine image are distinguished by their acts of mercy and their conduct of concern.

Entire sanctification brings stability of heart, enforcement against temptation and trial, strength for endurance. In His great high-priestly prayer Jesus prayed that the Father would send the Holy Spirit to "keep" or preserve His disciples (John 17:11-12). Entire sanctification, an establishing grace, is the answer to Christ's intercession for those who "believe on [him] through their word" (v. 20).

D. I. Vanderpool has said that the baptism of the Holy Spirit, or entire sanctification, does "heavy bridge and truss work" within man. "This is the experience that installs inside braces in strategic places. Thus the soul is fitted to bear heavy loads without caving in, and to stand heavy winds of temptation without folding up." This baptism "gives the soul an abiding Comforter for life's disappointments, a never-failing Guide for life's pilgrim journey . . . power for service anywhere in the church" or out of it.[12]

C. Divine Power and Cleansing

In Ephesians Paul highlighted the immeasurable resources that are available to the Christian. He stated that God has raised Jesus from the dead and exalted Him to the right hand of the Father, "far above all principality, and power, and might." Then he made the point that from the grave of our trespasses and sins, God has "raised us up together, and made us sit together in heavenly places in Christ Jesus" (1:20-21; 2:1, 5-6). That is, all the resources of heaven are available to those who live in the presence of God. The "exceeding greatness of his power to us-ward who believe" (1:19) is beyond human imagination and comprehension.

Yet "we have this treasure in jars of clay to show that this all-surpassing power is from God and not from us . . . so that the life of Jesus may . . . be revealed in our body" (2 Cor. 4:7, 10, NIV). Man is to be made the depository of God's Spirit, the very life of Christ lived out through him. Man's body—obviously in this life—is to be an effective instrument of Christian witness and service.

Entire sanctification enables one to live holy in this world. It has been pointed out that the words "pardon," "forgive," and "justify" occur approximately 194 times in the Scriptures, whereas the words "perfect," "upright," or "sanctify" occur over 990 times and are applied to the life we now live over 500 times.

John declared: "Love is made complete [perfect] among us so that we will have confidence on the day of judgment, because *in this world we are like him*" (1 John 4:17, NIV).

The Beloved Apostle unequivocally affirmed that not merely at or after death but *in this world* the entirely sanctified Christians are as their Master. He further stated that the blood of Christ "cleanseth" (not at the hour of death or in the day of judgment, but present tense)—at the present time—"from *all* sin" (1 John 1:7).

These great promises caused Wesley to admonish believers not to ask to "be renewed before you die. . . . Nay, but ask that it may be done now; today . . . Make haste, man, make haste! Let

Thy soul break out in strong desire
Thy perfect bliss to prove;
Thy longing heart be all on fire
To be dissolved in love!"[13]

"This is the will of God, even your [continuing] sanctification" (1 Thess. 4:3). "God hath not called us unto uncleanness, but unto [the life of] holiness" (v. 7). "And the
very God of peace sanctify you wholly [instantaneous—
entire sanctification]; and I pray God your whole spirit and
soul and body be preserved blameless unto the coming of
our Lord Jesus Christ. Faithful is he that calleth you, who
also will do it" (5:23-24).

ENTIRE SANCTIFICATION IS ENJOYED
IN A CERTAIN SPIRITUAL DETACHMENT

While the life of holiness is not withdrawal from the
needs of people around us, there is a kind of detachment
from everything that is secular, material, and temporal. It
is a life of spiritual fitness. It is keeping in shape so as to
make optimum use of one's potential to minister.

This understanding lay behind Susanna Wesley's wise
counsel to young John: "Whatever weakens your reason,
impairs the tenderness of your conscience, obscures your
sense of God, or takes off the relish of spiritual things,
whatever increases the authority of your body over your
mind, that thing for you is sin." A Spirit-controlled and
Spirit-disciplined life contributes to the social health of our
communities and neighborhoods.

In the holy life there is freedom from sin, so that man
does "abstain from all appearance [forms] of evil" (1 Thess.
5:22); there is also freedom from much that is legitimate,
but secondary. The entirely sanctified person will not allow
the good to rob him of God's best. Living a disciplined life,
he constantly prays: "Lord, put a thorn in every enjoy-

ment, a worm in every gourd that would retard my spiritual progress."

A. Keeping Our Priorities Straight

The entirely sanctified are willing to forgo some things that are not wrong in themselves because they demand time, energy, talent, or money that might be more wisely invested in God's service. It is in these areas that there is infinite room for growth and development in holiness. One of the great challenges and adventures of holy living is, to use the words of Harold Kuhn, "making the transition from character to practice—from that which the great and crucial experience of heart cleansing makes to be an *inner* reality to the outer realities of conduct which Christian sanctity implies."[14]

The detachment of which we are speaking is concerned with the constant fullness of the Spirit. The entirely sanctified Christian is not content to be cleansed from sin and separated from even the secondary things of life; he desires to be filled continuously with the Spirit. He wants to be rooted in Christ, filled with all the fullness of God. He hungers and thirsts for great grace, the abundant life, a relationship with God that brings power and perfects in love.

There is a fullness of the Spirit, says Daniel Steele, "which must imply entire sanctification—the permanent gracious presence in the soul of the Holy Spirit, in His fullness, not as an extraordinary gift, but as a person having the right-of-way through soul and body, having the keys to even the innermost rooms, illuminating every closet and permeating every crevice of the nature, filling the entire being with holy love."[15]

B. Continuing Growth in Grace (See Part I, pp. 27-28.)

Entire sanctification removes fundamental hindrances

to spiritual growth. In the life of holiness there is nurturing of the Christian graces, increase in bearing the fruit of the Spirit, an ever deepening of the spiritual life, increasing enjoyment of fellowship with God, strengthening of character, expanding of one's compassion and concern. Peter spoke of this growth specifically:

His divine power has given us everything we need for life and godliness through our knowledge of him who called us by his own *glory* and goodness. . . . For this very reason, make every effort to *add* to your faith goodness; and to goodness, knowledge; and to knowledge, self-control; and to self-control, perseverance; and to perseverance, godliness; and to godliness, brotherly kindness; and to brotherly kindness, love. For if you possess these qualities in *increasing measure,* they will keep you from being ineffective and unproductive in your knowledge of our Lord Jesus Christ. But if anyone does not have them, he is nearsighted and blind, and has forgotten that he has been *cleansed* from his past sins (*2 Pet. 1:3, 5-9, NIV*).

Because one is *attached* to Christ and *detached* from the secular, he is enabled to live victoriously in every vicissitude of life. Circumstances, though difficult, cannot overwhelm his spirit. By discipline and growth he is enabled to endure trials and afflictions and to live in the confidence that "in all things God works for the good of those who love him" (Rom. 8:28, NIV). It is a life of victory maintained moment by moment through active faith and obedience in Christ. There is a spiritual vitality that gives a fullness to life and a joyousness that is contagious.

C. Our Holy Fellowship

Though the entirely sanctified person enjoys a *personal* relationship with Christ, it is not an *individualized* relationship. A holy person knows that he is by grace a member of the Body of Christ. It is not insignificant that when the New Testament calls believers "saints" or "holy ones," it does so in the plural. Those who are truly living the holy life acknowledge that they are by virtue of being "in Christ" also a part of the fellowship of the saints (1 Cor. 12:12-27; Eph. 4:1-7).

Holiness is sustained by Christ's life, the life of the Church, the community of believers. There is "no solitary holiness." This truth Paul underscored with his proclamation that "Christ loved the church and gave himself up for her to make her holy, cleansing her by the washing with water through the word, . . . to present her to himself as a radiant church, without stain or wrinkle or any other blemish, but holy and blameless. . . . no one ever hated his own body, but he feeds and cares for it, just as Christ does the church—for we are members of his body" (Eph. 5:25-27, 29-30, NIV).

Conclusion

God's plan is for a holy people. The corporate body of Christian believers is the Body of Christ, His Church. The Church is holy in the sense that God through Christ has purchased and claimed it as His own, and also in the sense that there are Christians within the Church who are morally holy or pure in heart.[16] These Peter called a "holy nation" (1 Pet. 2:9), God's redeemed people, His instruments in accomplishing His redemptive purposes in history. The establishment of the Church is the fulfillment of the promise of the new covenant.

The divine scheme is fulfilled not only by the new covenant—the writing of God's law of love on man's heart —but also by the restoration of the divine image, begun in regeneration and continuing on to entire sanctification and beyond to glorification. "Beholding . . . the glory of the

Lord," God's holy people "are [being] changed into the same image . . . by the Spirit of the Lord" (2 Cor. 3:18). While the final transformation lies yet in the future, the Spirit effectively works now within Christ's followers, making them like Him.

Paul emphasized this increasing Christlikeness with his words: "That as sin hath reigned unto death, even so might grace reign through righteousness unto eternal life by Jesus Christ our Lord" (Rom. 5:12). That is, as sin unto death formerly reigned, so now through Christ, grace reigns—progressively, to the same extent, but more powerfully. "Where sin abounded, grace did much more abound" (v. 20)!

"In His likeness"—the legacy of every believer. Let us claim our inheritance, walk in obedience and faith, and pray with burning desire:

O to be like Thee, blessed Redeemer—
This is my constant longing and prayer.
Gladly I'll forfeit all of earth's treasures,
Jesus, Thy perfect likeness to wear.

O to be like Thee! while I am pleading,
Pour out Thy Spirit; fill with Thy love.
Make me a temple meet for Thy dwelling;
Fit me for life and heaven above.

O to be like Thee! O to be like Thee,
Blessed Redeemer, pure as Thou art!
Come in Thy sweetness, come in Thy fullness.
Stamp Thine own image deep on my heart.
                                        —THOMAS O. CHISHOLM

III

ALL LOVES EXCELLING

"'The heaven of heavens is love.' There is nothing higher in religion; there is, in effect, nothing else; if you look for anything but more love, you are looking wide of the mark, you are getting out of the royal way. And when you are asking others, 'Have you received this or that blessing?' if you mean anything but more love, you mean wrong; you are leading them out of the way, and putting them upon a false scent. Settle it then in your heart, that from the moment God has saved you from all sin, you are to aim at nothing more, but more of that love described in the thirteenth of the Corinthians. You can go no higher than this, till you are carried into Abraham's bosom."

—JOHN WESLEY
(*Works*, ed. Thomas Jackson, 11:430)

Our challenge as holiness preachers is underscored by the words of W. E. Sangster: "Nothing but an increase of saints will make the Church powerful in the world. . . . The Church is not despised because it is holy; it is despised because it is not holy enough."[1] Bishop Gerald Kennedy made the same point when he declared that the man on the street is looking for the marks of holiness on the church members.

As ministers, let us renew our covenant to preach holiness and challenge our people to look for and seek the blessing of entire sanctification made available through Christ's death and resurrection and by the gift of His Spirit. May we find joy in leading them into the "fullness of the blessing" and beyond, that they may love with the very love of Christ. Our focus must remain clear, namely, that "entire sanctification is neither more nor less than pure love; love expelling sin, and governing both the heart and life of the child of God. The Refiner's fire purges out all that is contrary to love."[2]

My prayer is that this simple holiness sermon, presented here in slightly more than skeletal form, may inspire your heart and mind as you minister in Christ's name and serve through the power of the sanctifying Spirit.

ALL LOVES EXCELLING

1 JOHN 4:10-21 (v. 17)

An Example of a Holiness Expositional Sermon

Introduction

God's love is the *definition* and *declaration* of pure love, by which all loves are to be evaluated and measured. It has been poured out on unworthy man and demonstrated in the propitiation for man's sins (v. 10).

The love of God in Christ "shed abroad in our hearts by the Holy [Spirit]" (Rom. 5:5; also see Titus 3:4-6) is the example that man is to emulate in all his personal and social relationships. This love alone is the *source* and *power* of all other loves.

John Wesley equated this love of God in man with holiness and holy living. He taught that "Christian perfection," or "perfect love," is "loving God with all the heart, soul, mind, and strength, and one's neighbor as oneself."

The validity of Wesley's judgment is borne out by the passage before us. The purpose of the entire Epistle is seen in such expressions as: "that ye may know that ye have eternal life" (5:13); "that ye sin not" (2:1); "that your joy may be full" (1:4). John's aim is to direct believers into the *fullness* of God's love. He does this by portraying his vision of Christian holiness, which is perfect love for God and man.

This Epistle, then, is one of love, holiness, and the victorious life. It reflects a deep, vital union with God, emphasizing true holiness and righteousness. The disciple whom Jesus loved combines his understanding of *life in God* and the *life of perfect love* with the *fullness of the Spirit*.

Chapter 4, verse 17, and the surrounding verses, present to Christ's followers the biblical standard of *perfect*

147

love revealed in and made possible by Jesus Christ. The emphasis is not so much on the stages or crises of faith and experience through which one passes to come to this degree of maturity; but rather on the quality of life that results from the divine activity exercised in saving and sanctifying grace. What we have here is a description of the life of holiness and of the possibilities of Christlikeness through the fullness of the indwelling Spirit.

Our passage of Scripture clearly describes and reflects the character of one whose love has been *made perfect*. In these 12 verses the word "love" is used 22 times. The English word "love" translates two different words in the New Testament that convey different meanings. One *(agapē)* is used primarily to refer to God's love and refers to a deep and constant love that is not dependent upon the merit of its object. The other *(philia)* represents the tender affection between two human beings. In all 22 instances the former word is used. Thus we are talking about God's kind of love.

Three tests of divine life or perfect love are put forward in John's Epistle:

1. Whether we believe that Jesus is the Son of God—by the commitment of our will
2. Whether we are living lives of righteousness—moral and ethical uprightness
3. Whether we have love one for another—even for our enemies

When asked, "Is there any example in Scripture of persons who have attained perfect love?" Wesley replied: "Yes, St. John and all those of whom he speaks in 1 John 4:17."

Let us look at the way the apostle of love views a "true" Christian, one who is filled with perfect love. May we ask ourselves: Do we love with a love made perfect—

with the very love of Christ? And may we pray with
Charles Wesley:

> *Love divine, **all loves excelling,***
> *Joy of heav'n, to earth come down!*
> *Fix in us Thy humble dwelling;*
> *All Thy faithful mercies crown.*
> *Jesus, Thou art all compassion;*
> *Pure, unbounded love Thou art.*
> *Visit us with Thy salvation;*
> *Enter ev'ry trembling heart.*
> (emphasis added)

I. Perfect Love Excels in the Fellowship It Preserves (1:3-7)

First John has all the marks of a sermon, the work of a
pastor who seeks to build up his people in the faith. The
author employs graphic contrasts—light and darkness, life
and death, saint and sinner, love and hate, Christ and An-
tichrist. These contrasts are practically synonymous, and
any one of them may be substituted by almost any other.
They can all be expressed in the phrase "fellowship and
alienation." John is extolling "fellowship," the immediate
union of the soul with God that issues in righteousness in
all the relationships of one's life. Perfect love both creates
and preserves this fellowship.

A. This Fellowship Is a Gift of God Through Jesus Christ (v. 10)

Sinful man cannot love God or have fellowship with
Him ("Not that we loved God"). We were enemies to God,
and yet Christ died for us. It was God's love, not our merit
or our lovableness, that induced Him to devise means to
accomplish our salvation.

"We love him, because he first loved us" (v. 19). God's
love for man is not a response to our love. Our love de-

pends upon, and is the result of, His love. Real love in its
origin is not human but divine. Human love at best is only
responsive; it is never original and spontaneous. The mar-
vel of God's method with men is that He loves them into
loving—both by His prevenient grace and by His trans-
forming grace. In this His love excels.

B. *This Fellowship Is Made Possible by the Removal of Our
Sins (v. 10)*

The Father has "sent his Son to be the propitiation for
our sins." The Greek word for "propitiation" is used only
here and in 2:2, without reference to the one to whom it is
offered. It should not be understood as an appeasement to
God but as a reference to the personal means by whom
God shows mercy to those who believe on Christ. Thus the
word has been rendered an "atoning sacrifice" (NIV).

In and through Christ man finds mercy and forgiveness of his sins, pardon and peace with God. The alienation and estrangement that separated man from God are
taken away. The guilt and power of sin that weighted
down man and held him in bondage are gone. One is reconciled to God by Christ's death, a "new and living way"
whereby we have access to the Father (Heb. 10:19-20). The
pollution of sin, the spirit of selfishness that hinders
growth in grace, is cleansed. In dealing effectively with the
sin problem, God's perfect love excels.

C. *This Fellowship Rests upon Confession of Christ as Savior and Lord (vv. 14-15)*

The testimony described, "we have seen and do testify," expresses the common and abiding witness of the
Church (cf. 1:1-5) as it is appropriated by the faith of each
believer personally. The confession "that Jesus is the Son of
God" is not merely the mental assent to, nor declaration of,
a fact—even the devils have this kind of faith and "trem-
ble" (James 2:19). Rather, it is the public recognition and

acceptance of the person of Christ as the Divine Savior. It is submission to Him as Lord and trust in Him for salvation. He who with the heart thus acknowledges Him, and with the tongue confesses Him, receives Him and has eternal life (cf. Rom. 10:9-10).

"God dwelleth in him" who makes this confession, "and he in God" (v. 15). This reciprocal indwelling in God and in Christ implies the most intimate fellowship of the believer with the Father and with the Son, in whom He is revealed. The conditions of this fellowship are love, confession, and obedience. The effects are fruitfulness and acceptance. The sign is the possession of the Holy Spirit, who lavishes God's love in the heart and inspires the filial feeling, so that we may pray, "Abba, Father" (Rom. 8:15; Gal. 4:6). To so recognize the Father and His working, which is a result of God's grace, certifies true sonship.

Perfect love preserves this fellowship—in this it excels.

II. *Perfect Love Excels in the Assurance It Provides (v. 7)*

One cannot gain acceptance with God through good deeds or accumulated merit, by one's economic or racial background—but by grace alone through faith in Jesus Christ. The apostle Paul failed to find peace with God through his own righteousness. He was circumcised the eighth day, of the stock of Israel, of the tribe of Benjamin, a Hebrew of the Hebrews, a Pharisee. He zealously persecuted the Church, a virtue in the minds of the Jews. Regarding the law, he was blameless. His dependence upon these "virtues" only increased his guilt and magnified his spiritual paucity. But when he met Jesus Christ on the Damascus road and accepted His righteousness, his life was transformed, and he was accepted into "the beloved." He testified to the Philippians: "What things were gain to me, those I counted loss for Christ" (3:7).

A. God Assures That We Belong to Him by Giving His Spirit of Love (v. 13)

The source of the Christian's assurance is the Gift of the Holy Spirit (see 3:24; also Rom. 8:15-16). Here is the Divine Presence whom Jesus said He would ask the Father to send His disciples and all His followers of every age (John 14:16). The Holy Spirit brings assurance to the Christian because the devil has been judged, and all who dwell in God, and God in him, share in the victory over evil (John 16:11).

The Holy Spirit is the Christian's proof of acceptance with God. His presence enables him to know that he belongs to God. The Spirit is the evidence of the fellowship of the community of Christ's Body, because all experience the same Presence. While the Holy Spirit respects and enhances each one's individuality, there is a oneness about His presence that assures each member of a common fellowship through Him. That oneness is the unity of their faith in Jesus Christ. This confession is prompted by the indwelling Spirit.

It is for this reason that the Spirit centers attention upon Jesus. When we say we "feel the Spirit," we mean we are sensing the presence of Christ. When the Spirit indwells us, He enables us to exalt Christ, a confirmation that we belong to Him.

B. God Gives Assurance, or "Boldness," for the Day of Judgment—Through Christlikeness (v. 17)

To live in the love of God and have it flow out of us to others bears fruit in holy boldness. The fear of judgment fades because one sees in the person of our Judge Him who has died for us, regenerated our hearts, and fills us with himself. The writer of Hebrews expresses a virtually universal anxiety of mankind when he says that all men must die and after this face the Judgment (9:27). Whether that Judgment be the Great White Throne (Rev. 20:11-15) or the judgment of consequences in this 'life, it is a fearful thing.

The love of God in one's heart brings boldness because one knows the Judge of all is working out His purpose in one's life. This boldness comes because that one is becoming like Christ, the Standard by which all men are judged. What will be asked of the believer at the last is already occurring through the cleansing and empowering love of God in the heart and life of the child of God. The love of God makes one fearless of judgment, because judgment is that which is happening in the person in whom the love of God is perfected.

John firmly declares, "As he is"—pure, holy, loving— "so are we in this world" (v. 17)—saved from our sins, made like to himself "in righteousness and true holiness" (Eph. 4:24). The ground of our boldness, then, is present likeness to Christ. Our essential likeness to Him is not in our trials, or persecutions, or sufferings, nor even primarily in the fact that we are not of the world as He is not of the world. Rather, it is in the fact that we are *righteous* as He is *righteous*. Our likeness is to Christ's character and spirit.

C. Perfect Love Casts Out Fear (v. 18)

There is "no fear in love" because fear pulls apart, while love unites. Love that is *perfect* casts out fear. Fear has to do with God's punishment and is an aspect of His discipline—"fear hath torment." The one who fears is not perfected in love and therefore shrinks away from God.

Bengel has said there are four classes of men:

1. Those who have *neither fear nor love*—the unregenerate and unconverted. They have no love for God and no fear of God.

2. Those who have *fear of God,* but *no love for Him*—the unregenerate but now convicted. They have caught a glimpse of their sinfulness and are afraid.

3. Those who have *both fear and love*—the newly regenerated, babes in Christ, or young converts. They love God but still fear Him because of their inner uncleanness.

4. Those who have *only love for God*—Christians in whom the love of God is perfected. They have had their heart cleansed from all inward sin and have been sanctified wholly (to use our terminology).

Someone asked Dr. J. G. Morrison: "How much religion will a man have to have to make it to heaven?" He replied: "Enough that he feels comfortable in the presence of a holy God." That requires a holy heart.

"Perfect love casteth out fear."

We must not suppose that the love of God implanted in the heart of man is ever imperfect in itself; it is only so in degree. But there may be a lesser or greater degree of what is perfect in itself. So it is with respect to the love that the followers of Christ have. We are not to imagine that the love of God casts out *every* kind of fear from the soul—fear of falling from great heights, fear of fire, and so on. But perfect love does cast out that fear that has "torment"— fear of God himself. We stand in awe of Him and with reverence, but we do not cringe before Him in fear of capricious judgment.

The more one grows in the Christian graces, the more other kinds of fear are removed: fear of failure, fear that others will betray, fear of people's opinions. Such fears distort perspective, disrupt relationships, retard growth, and inhibit development. There are fears that blind moral judgment and inflame passions.

Love is positive; fear is negative. These are mutually

exclusive. The more one loves, the less he fears. The more he fears, the less he loves. While some fears may have value, "There is nothing that fear does for us in a constructive way that love and confidence will not do better" (T. E. Martin). Perfect love enables us to accept each day, and all that it brings, in confidence and boldness. In this it excels.

III. Perfect Love Excels in the Service It Promotes (vv. 7-8, 11, 20-21)

A. *Love for Others Is Rooted in Love for God, or Love from God (v. 21)*

"If God so loved us, we ought also to love one another" (v. 11). We are to love those who are a part of the fellowship of believers. However, Jesus told the disciples that if they loved only those who loved them, they would have no reward (Matt. 5:46). This includes loving one's enemies and doing good to those who persecute us (vv. 43-45). Loving others, even our enemies, is not so tall an order when we see the activity of God in us. The love we have for God and others comes from the indwelling presence of God. God dwells in those who love Him, and His love is perfected in them. Perfect love is the work of God in the heart of the believer. It is the nature of God not only to love but also to bring that love to perfection or fulfillment. Christian holiness is the fruit of the love relationship with God. It is what He intends for everyone born again of the Spirit.

The initiative, of course, is God's. We do not perfect His love in us; He does. When we open our hearts to the love of God in commitment, consecration, faith, and obedience, we are at one with the purpose for which we were created. We begin to be what we were intended to be. That intention is brought to fulfillment as His love is perfected in us. Having this perfection of love, one can see God. Jesus said, "Blessed are the pure in heart: for they shall see [enjoy] God" (Matt. 5:8). This perfection or purity of heart is an unselfish and giving love that does not love for return but finds its joy in giving.

B. *Hatred, or Unconcern for Others, Evidences a Lack of Perfect Love (v. 20)*

John asks a pointed rhetorical question: If one does not love "his brother whom he hath seen, how can he love God whom he hath not seen?" The implication is that if a man fails in the duty of love to one with whom he is in daily interaction, he cannot perform the more difficult duty of loving one whom he has never seen and whose existence is invisible to him except by the eye of faith. To this point, John has not directly mentioned our love for God. Now he brings it into sharp focus and insists that our love for God is validated by our love for others.

Loving others, with a love made perfect, is not an option but a commandment: "This commandment . . . That he who loveth God love his brother also" (v. 21). This may be a reference to the summary of the Mosaic law that calls for loving God with one's whole heart and one's neighbor as oneself (Lev. 19:18; Deut. 6:5; Matt. 22:37-39; Mark 12:30-31; Luke 10:27). The commandment is a commandment of love. Love, being of the very nature of God, contains its own motivation to self-expression toward others. It is of the nature of God's love in us to express itself. The proof that love is real, *perfected*, in the full Christian sense, lies in the overt action to which it leads. There is no real love for God that does not show itself in obedience to His commands—love being lived out to its "fingertips" in all segments of our society. In this perfect love excels.

Conclusion

The *beauty* of this passage of Scripture is rivaled only by 1 Cor. 13—the "hymn of love." "God is love" (v. 16). He has made His love known to man through His Son, awakening man's echoing response, which is demonstrated in visible acts of service to others.

The question is: Has the *beauty* of this perfected love come to decorate our lives? Have we confessed our lack of love and consecrated our life to God? Do we in this moment love God with all our heart, soul, mind, and strength, and our neighbor (as well as enemies) as ourselves?

If not, we can by His grace. His love can be implanted in our hearts by the fullness of the Holy Spirit. We may by faith receive Him who is Love, enabling and empowering us to love "because he first loved us."

> *"Herein is our love made perfect."*
> *All other loves this love excels.*

APPENDIX

We Believe:

"the doctrine and experience of sanctification as a *second* work of grace;

"that . . . God . . . is holy in nature, attributes, and purpose;

"in the Holy Spirit, . . . that He is ever present and efficiently active in and with the Church of Christ . . . , regenerating those who repent and believe, sanctifying believers, and guiding into all truth as it is in Jesus;

"that original sin continues to exist with the new life of the regenerate, until eradicated by the baptism with the Holy Spirit;

"that Jesus Christ, by His sufferings, by the shedding of His own blood, and by His meritorious death on the Cross, made a *full* atonement for *all* human sin, and that this atonement is the *only* ground of salvation . . . ;

"that entire sanctification is that act of God, *subsequent to regeneration,* by which believers are made free from original sin, or depravity, and brought into a state of entire devotement to God, and the holy obedience of love made perfect . . . ;

"It is wrought by the baptism of the Holy Spirit, and comprehends in one experience the *cleansing* of the heart from sin and the abiding indwelling presence of the Holy Spirit, *empowering* the believer for life and service . . . ;

"Entire sanctification is provided by the blood of Jesus, is wrought *instantaneously* by faith, preceded by entire consecration; and to this work and state of grace the Holy Spirit bears witness . . . ;

"This experience is also known by various terms representing its different phases, such as 'Christian perfection,' 'perfect love,' 'heart purity,' 'the baptism with the Holy Spirit,' 'the fullness of the blessing,' and 'Christian holiness.'"[1]

Steps to Holiness

I. INITIAL SANCTIFICATION (conversion); justification, regeneration, adoption
   A. Repentance—confession and forsaking of all past sins, known and unknown
   B. Restitution—making right all wrongs, insofar as one is capable, and in cases where others will not be hurt by your action
   C. Faith—acceptance of God's promise of forgiveness, and a trusting commitment of oneself to God; reliance upon God's mercy rather than upon one's own merit
   D. Witness of the Spirit—God's Spirit bearing witness with your spirit that you are a child of God, a new creature in Christ
   E. Walking in the light—day-by-day obedience to God and faithfulness to His service. There will be a growing consciousness of an inner foe that hinders one's witness and insists on one having his own selfish way.

II. ENTIRE SANCTIFICATION (cleansing of the sin nature and infilling of the Holy Spirit)
   A. Clear knowledge of one's conversion—consciousness that one is accepted by God and is not disobedient to His commands
   B. Increasing hunger and thirst for God—acknowledgment of one's need for complete cleansing from in-being sin, and a growing desire for one's will to be brought into perfect alignment with the will of God
   C. Avoidance of all that would damage one's influence for God—a willingness to give up even legitimate things if they limit one's service to God and others
   D. Definite seeking for the blessing—an expression of one's determination to be wholly God's
   E. Consecration—a once-for-all yielding up to God of one's redeemed self—time, talent, treasure, past, present, and future; total abandonment to God
   F. Appropriating faith—acceptance of God's gift of the fullness of the Spirit, allowing Him to control and direct the life without reservation

III. CONTINUING SANCTIFICATION (growth in grace)
   A. Continuous walking in the light—acknowledgment of failure or omissions; praise to God for all things good; glad acceptance of His will and leadership
   B. Cultivation by grace of the virtues of Christ; a life of joy, radiance, peace, victory
   C. Expanding sensitivity to one's social obligations and opportunities to express God's love to others
IV. FINAL SANCTIFICATION (glorification)
   A. Gift of a perfect, glorified body, like the resurrected body of Christ
   B. Complete restoration of all that was lost in the fall of Adam

Glossary of Terms

GENERAL HOLINESS TERMS

1. *Baptism with the Holy Spirit*—a broad term that includes entire sanctification, the moral cleansing of the heart, but emphasizes the positive activity of God—empowering for service, etc.
2. *Christian perfection*—sometimes used synonymously with entire sanctification; however, generally refers to the life—both attitude and action—of holiness
3. *Fullness of the Spirit*—stresses the abiding presence of God within the life of the believer; emphasizes the progressive and continuous aspect of the Spirit-filled life. There is one baptism in the sense of instantaneous cleansing and empowering, though there are "many fillings."
4. *Holy*—the condition of being set apart for the service of God—both persons and things; the condition or state of being morally pure, free from sin
5. *Holiness*—expresses the condition or quality of that which is holy; the consequence of being sanctified; generally refers to the life of holiness
6. *Sanctify*—(1) to make sacred or holy; to set apart to a holy use; to consecrate by appropriate rites; to hallow

(2) to make free from sin; to cleanse from moral corruption or pollution; to purify

7. *Sanctification*—the act and/or process by which one is made holy; that activity of God by which the affections of men are purified from sin and exalted to a supreme love to God

8. *Sanctification (initial)*—the washing or cleansing from the *guilt* of sin; the beginning of the life of holiness, simultaneous with regeneration

9. *Sanctification (entire)*—the washing or cleansing from the *pollution* or spirit of sin, subsequent to regeneration; that act of God wrought instantaneously by faith in which the believer is purged of the sinful self and filled with the love of God

10. *Sanctification (continuing)*—moment-by-moment cleansing conditioned upon moment-by-moment obedience and faith; the continuing activity of God within the Christian, enabling him to progress and grow in the life of holiness

11. *Perfect love*—expressive of the spirit and temper, or moral atmosphere, in which the wholly sanctified live (J. A. Wood); undivided allegiance to the will of God and active seeking of the well-being of others, even one's enemies

TERMS RELATED TO HOLINESS

1. *Adoption*—that act of God whereby one is brought into the family of God and given all rights, privileges, and inheritances of sonship. Takes place at conversion.

2. *Atonement*—God's reconciling work accomplished in the death of His Son at Calvary

3. *Carnal mind*—the spirit of lawlessness in man; inordinate selfishness that is not subject to the law of God; a spirit contrary to the spirit of Christ

4. *Consecration*—man's act of setting himself apart to God, though he is enabled by God's grace. While every person seeking salvation makes a full commitment to God insofar as he is able and conscious, technically this is an act of a regenerated person.

5. *Depravity*—denotes the sinful perversion of man's nature, which affects every member of the human family; defile-

ment, corruption, or spirit of degeneracy, which yet remains following one's conversion

6. *Eradication*—that act of God whereby the in-being of sin is removed, destroyed, cleansed. While the word is not found in the English Bible, it expresses the biblical meanings of "crucified," "put off," "purged," "take away," and so on.

7. *Glorification*—perfection of the body given to man at the last day, and patterned after the resurrected body of Christ

8. *Infirmities*—refers to man's impaired natural powers, resulting from the fall of man and from man's sinful conduct. They sometimes occasion errors, mistakes in judgment, or wrong actions. While these "shortcomings" are not, strictly speaking, sin, they need the forgiveness of Christ and the covering of His atonement.

9. *Justification*—that act of God whereby man is pardoned of his sins and accepted by God. Occurs at conversion to God.

10. *Original sin*—describes the source of one's sins, that defilement of nature that gives rise to outward manifestations of sin; also called "inbred" or "birth" sin

11. *Regeneration*—that act of God whereby man is made new, born from above or of the Spirit, raised from the death of sin to new life in Christ. Simultaneous with justification and adoption.

12. *Sin (sins)*—outward actions or inward attitudes incurring guilt, requiring forgiveness or pardon

13. *Sin (sinfulness)*—pollution, or a spirit of lawlessness, which insists on one's own way, requiring cleansing

Other Terms Used in This Study

1. *Immanence*—when applied to God, it refers to His nearness, His accessibility, His pervading presence among men and in history.

2. *Soteriology*—from two Greek terms meaning "salvation" and "the study of." Thus the "study of salvation" as provided and effected by Christ.

3. *Transcendence*—when applied to God, it refers to His majesty, His glory, His "otherness" from man. His power and purity transcend man's comprehension.

NOTES

PART I
Chapter 1

1. Oswald Chambers, *Conformed to His Image* (Fort Washington, Pa.: Christian Literature Crusade, 1950), 37.

2. Oswald Chambers, *God's Workmanship* (Fort Washington, Pa.: Christian Literature Crusade, 1953), 48.

3. Richard S. Taylor, *Preaching Holiness Today* (Kansas City: Beacon Hill Press of Kansas City, 1968), 14.

4. See E. Stanley Jones, *Is the Kingdom of God Realism?* (New York: Abingdon-Cokesbury Press, 1940); also *The Unshakable Kingdom and the Unchanging Person* (Nashville: Abingdon Press, 1972).

5. Taylor, *Preaching Holiness,* chap. 1.

6. Quoted in William M. Greathouse, *The Fullness of the Spirit* (Kansas City: Nazarene Publishing House, 1958), preface.

7. Gideon B. Williamson, *Preaching Scriptural Holiness* (Kansas City: Beacon Hill Press, 1953), preface.

Chapter 2

1. John Wesley, "The Circumcision of the Heart," in *Wesley's Standard Sermons,* ed. Edward H. Sugden (London: Epworth Press, 1921), 1:273. Cited hereafter as *WSS.*

2. Mildred Bangs Wynkoop, "The Preaching of Holiness" (unpublished article, 1968). Also see her *Theology of Love* (Kansas City: Beacon Hill Press of Kansas City, 1972).

3. Ibid.

4. John Wesley, "A Plain Account of Christian Perfection," in *The Works of John Wesley,* ed. Thomas Jackson, 3rd ed., 14 vols. (London: Wesleyan Methodist Book Room, 1872; reprint, Kansas City: Beacon Hill Press of Kansas City, 1978-79), 11:387. Hereafter cited as *WJW.*

5. *Manual of the Church of the Nazarene* 1993-97, par. 13, 30-31.

6. For a discussion of some of these "common misconceptions" see Part II, chap. 7.

7. Basic texts that John Wesley used in the preaching of holiness:

(1) Ezek. 36:25-26, 29	(9) 2 Cor. 3:17 ff.
(2) Matt. 5:8	(10) 2 Cor. 7:1
(3) Matt. 5:48	(11) Gal. 2:20
(4) Matt. 6:10	(12) Eph. 3:14-19
(5) John 8:34 ff.	(13) Eph. 5:27
(6) John 17:20-23	(14) Phil. 3:15
(7) Rom. 2:29	(15) 1 Thess. 5:23
(8) Rom. 12:1	(16) Titus 2:11-14

(17) Heb. 6:1	(24) 1 John 2:12-15
(18) Heb. 7:25	(25) 1 John 2:25-29
(19) Heb. 10:14	(26) 1 John 3:3
(20) James 1:4	(27) 1 John 3:8-10
(21) 1 John 1:5, 7	(28) 1 John 4:12-13
(22) 1 John 1:8-9	(29) 1 John 4:17-18
(23) 1 John 2:5-6	(30) 1 John 5:13-21

For a slightly different listing see W. E. Sangster, *The Path to Perfection* (New York: Abingdon-Cokesbury Press, 1943), 37-52.

8. *Manual,* par. 14, 31.

PART II
Chapter 3

1. Norman H. Snaith, *Distinctive Ideas of the Old Testament* (London: Epworth Press, 1944), 22.

2. Ibid., 30.

3. A. B. Davidson, *The Theology of the Old Testament* (Edinburgh: T. and T. Clark, 1904), 152.

4. D. Shelby Corlett, *The Meaning of Holiness* (Kansas City: Beacon Hill Press, 1944), 14.

5. Asbury Lowrey, *Possibilities of Grace* (Boston: Christian Witness Co., 1884), 103.

6. R. F. Weidmer, *Biblical Theology of the Old Testament* (Minneapolis: Augustana Book Co., n.d.), 72.

7. Emil Brunner, *The Christian Doctine of God* (London: Lutterworth Press, 1949), 1:164.

8. H. Orton Wiley and Paul T. Culbertson, *An Introduction to Christian Theology* (Kansas City: Beacon Hill Press, 1946), 105.

9. T. C. Vriezen, *An Outline of Old Testament Theology* (Newton, Mass.: Charles T. Branford Co., 1960), 141.

10. George Allen Turner, *The Vision Which Transforms* (Kansas City: Beacon Hill Press of Kansas City, 1964), 120.

11. Paul Gray, "Jeremiah," in *Beacon Bible Commentary* (Kansas City: Beacon Hill Press of Kansas City, 1966), 4:430.

Chapter 4

1. The Bible occasionally refers to the "face of God" (Lev. 17:10; Num. 6:25), to the "arm of the LORD" (Exod. 6:6; Job 40:9; Ps. 89:13), to God's "hand" (Judg. 2:15; Isa. 59:1), to the "eye of the LORD" (2 Chron. 16:9; Ps. 33:18), and so on. These expressions are called anthropomorphisms, accommodations to man's limited understanding and illustrations of his inability to describe that which is infinite.

2. J. B. Chapman, *The Terminology of Holiness* (Kansas City: Beacon Hill Press, 1947), 24.

3. Brunner, *Christian Doctrine of God,* 2:93.

4. Wiley and Culbertson, *Introduction to Christian Theology,* 164-65.

5. *WSS,* Sugden, ed., 1:188, 183.

6. For a discussion of these theories, see H. Orton Wiley, *Christian Theology,* 3 vols. (Kansas City: Beacon Hill Press, 1940-43), 2:109-19.

7. John Wesley, *The Doctrine of Original Sin* (New York: J. Soule and T. Mason, 1817), 97, 313.

8. *WJW,* 9:335.

9. W. T. Purkiser, *Beliefs That Matter Most* (Kansas City: Nazarene Publishing House, 1959), 44.

Chapter 5

1. For good summaries and discussions on which I here depend, see Donald Metz, *Studies in Biblical Holiness* (Kansas City: Beacon Hill Press of Kansas City, 1971), 56-70; and Turner, *Vision Which Transforms,* 27-32, 98-114.

2. Snaith, *Distinctive Ideas of the Old Testament,* 66.

3. Turner, *Vision Which Transforms,* 30.

4. Ibid., 104.

5. Ibid., 105.

6. *WJW,* 12:394, 11:395-96.

7. W. T. Purkiser, *Conflicting Concepts of Holiness* (Kansas City: Beacon Hill Press, 1953), 51.

8. Merne A. Harris and Richard S. Taylor, "The Dual Nature of Sin," in *The Word and the Doctrine,* ed. Kenneth Geiger (Kansas City: Beacon Hill Press of Kansas City, 1965), 96.

9. Paragraphs immediately following are taken by permission from John A. Knight, *The Holiness Pilgrimage* (Kansas City: Beacon Hill Press of Kansas City, 1973), 86-88.

10. Harris and Taylor, *Word and the Doctrine,* 108.

Chapter 6

1. D. M. Baillie, *God Was in Christ* (New York: Charles Scribner's Sons, 1948), 194.

2. A. H. Strong, *Systematic Theology* (Westwood, N.J.: Fleming H. Revell Co., 1907), 266.

3. R. S. Taylor, *A Right Conception of Sin* (Kansas City: Beacon Hill Press, 1945), 92.

4. Ibid., 96.

5. Ibid., 99-100.

6. Wiley, *Christian Theology,* 1:383.

7. Lowrey, *Possibilities of Grace,* 179.

8. F. C. Grant, *An Introduction to New Testament Thought* (New York: Abingdon-Cokesbury Press, 1950), 184.

9. Ralph Earle, "The Nature and Extent of the Atonement," in Geiger, *Word and the Doctrine,* 175.

10. James Stewart, *A Man in Christ* (New York: Harper and Bros., n.d.), 152-53.

11. Friedrich Buechsel, "*Katallassō* (Reconciliation) in the New Testament," in *Theological Dictionary of the New Testament,* ed. Gerhard Kittel, trans. G. W. Bromiley (Grand Rapids: Wm. B. Eerdmans Publishing Co., 1964), 1:255.

12. Knight, *Holiness Pilgrimage,* 34.

13. Wiley, *Christian Theology,* 2:464.

14. Knight, *Holiness Pilgrimage,* 36f.

15. Earle, *Word and the Doctrine,* 177. I am indebted to Dr. Earle for his excellent article and for several of the references used in this chapter.

16. Delbert R. Rose (quoting Paul S. Rees), "Entirely the Lord's," in *The Holiness Pulpit, No. 2,* comp. James McGraw (Kansas City: Beacon Hill Press of Kansas City, 1974), 36.

17. T. A. Hegre has observed that the apostle Paul did not explicitly mention "sin" (singular) in the first chapters of Romans. From 1:1 to 5:11 he spoke only of "sins" (plural). From 5:12 on he referred only to "sin" in the singular. "It is also significant," says Hegre, "that in the first section of Romans in connection with *sins,* Paul (spoke) of the blood of Christ but never of the Cross. On the contrary, in the last section Paul never (mentioned) the blood of Christ but only the Cross of Christ." The distinction may be a bit artificial, but Hegre is suggesting that the blood of Christ deals with sins committed, whereas the Cross deals with sinfulness of nature. See Hegre, *How to Find Freedom from the Power of Sin* (Minneapolis: Bethany Fellowship, 1961), 66-67.

18. This discussion relies in part on an unpublished paper by W. M. Greathouse, "The Dynamics of Sanctification: Biblical Terminology," read at the Nazarene Theology Conference, Kansas City, Dec. 4-6, 1969.

19. T. A. Hegre, *The Cross and Sanctification* (Minneapolis: Bethany Fellowship, 1960), 14.

20. Greathouse, "The Dynamics of Sanctification," 18.

Chapter 7

1. Knight, *Holiness Pilgrimage,* 92-93.

2. G. B. Williamson, "Re-created in the Image of God," in *The Holiness Pulpit,* comp. James McGraw (Kansas City: Beacon Hill Press, 1957), 29.

3. W. M. Greathouse, *The Fullness of the Spirit* (Kansas City: Nazarene Publishing House, 1958), 96.

4. H. V. Miller, *The Sin Problem* (Kansas City: Beacon Hill Press, 1947), 71.

5. Greathouse, *Fullness of the Spirit,* 11.

6. Wiley, *Christian Theology,* 2:441.

7. Daniel Steele, *Love Enthroned* (New York: Nelson and Phillips, 1877), 29.

8. Rose, *Holiness Pulpit, No. 2,* 40.

9. Sangster, *Path to Perfection,* 52.

10. Wiley, *Christian Theology,* 2:444.

11. George Lyons has stated: "Too much has been made of the aorist tense in holiness interpretation of passages . . . Greek grammar alone is an insufficient basis for defending the view that entire sanctification begins in a crisis moment subsequent to regeneration. An earlier generation of holiness-traditions scholars (e.g., Daniel Steele and Olive Winchester) overstated the grammatical evidence for entire sanctification as a 'second definite work of grace.' For appropriate cautions against overdependence on such arguments see Robert W. Lyon, 'The Baptism of the Spirit—Continued,' *Wesleyan Theological Journal* 15, no. 2 (1980): 70-74; and Randy Maddox, 'The Use of the Aorist Tense in Holiness Exegesis,' *Wesleyan Theological Journal* 16, no. 2 (1981): 106-18" (George Lyons, *Holiness in Everyday Life* [Kansas City: Beacon Hill Press of Kansas City, 1992], 48, n. 3). On the other hand, J. Kenneth Grider, in spite of certain "reservations," still insists that the aorist tense is "in some contexts supportive of entire sanctification's instantaneousness." However, he acknowledges that the context in some cases must determine the interpretation. See his *Wesleyan-Holiness Theology* (Kansas City: Beacon Hill Press of Kansas City, 1994), 395-96.

12. Lyons acknowledges that the verb "offer" in Rom. 12:1-2 (NIV) implies a decisive act of permanent commitment. But it is the imagery of sacrifice that justifies this statement rather than the aorist tense of the verb (Lyons, *Holiness in Everyday Life*, 48).

13. W. M. Greathouse, *Romans*, vol. 6 of *Beacon Bible Expositions* (Kansas City: Beacon Hill Press of Kansas City, 1975), 106.

14. Fulton J. Sheen, "The Psychology of Conversion," in *Peace of Soul* (New York: McGraw-Hill, 1940), 236-43.

15. *The Works of the Rev. John Fletcher*, 4 vols. (New York: Phillips and Hunt, 1883), 4:113-14. Cited hereafter as *FW*.

16. *WJW*, 8:328.

17. I am indebted to Jack Ford both for this idea and the phraseology. See his *What the Holiness People Believe* (Lowestoft, England: Green and Co., n.d.), 62-63.

18. Paul Rees in his Glide Lectures given at Asbury Theological Seminary, *Asbury Seminarian* (spring 1948): 11 ff. Quoted in Ford, *What the Holiness People Believe*, 61.

19. Ford, *What the Holiness People Believe*, 62-64.

20. *WJW*, 11:419; see also 6:412.

21. Ibid., 11:428.

22. This helpful principle was suggested by Ponder Gilliland in an unpublished paper, "Problems of Failure in the Sanctified Life," read to Nazarene Theology Conference, Kansas City, Dec. 4-6, 1969.

Chapter 8

1. Wiley, *Christian Theology*, 2:479.

2. *Wesley's Explanatory Notes upon the New Testament*, 1 John 4:18.

3. These are borrowed from W. E. Sangster's summary of the basic teachings of John Wesley (which we believe to have biblical foundation) concerning holiness, entire sanctification, or Christian perfection.

4. *WJW*, 6:45, 46.

5. Ibid., 11:394.

6. Ibid., 6:45.

7. Ibid., 50-51.

8. *FW*, 4:431.

9. It is frequently pointed out that entire sanctification is analogous to the new birth, which is wrought instantaneously within the believer: Both are expressions of divine love (John 3:16; Eph. 5:25-27); both are subjects of God's will (1 Thess. 4:3; 1 Tim. 2:3-4); both are accomplished through the Word of God (John 17:17; 1 Pet. 1:23); both are executed by the Holy Spirit (2 Thess. 2:13; Titus 3:5); both are provided by Christ's atonement (Rom. 5:9; Heb. 13:12); both are by grace and not works (Eph. 2:8-9; Titus 2:11-14); both are by faith (Acts 15:8-9; Rom. 5:1). See W. T. Purkiser, ed., *Exploring Our Christian Faith* (Kansas City: Beacon Hill Press, 1960), 354-56.

10. *WSS*, 2:459-60.

11. Ibid., 1:208, 226-27. See also 2:343-44.

12. D. I. Vanderpool, "The Baptism with the Holy Ghost," in McGraw, *Holiness Pulpit, No. 2*, 32-33.

13. *WJW*, 11:403.

14. Harold B. Kuhn, "Ethics and the Holiness Movement," in *Insights into*

Holiness, comp. Kenneth Geiger (Kansas City: Beacon Hill Press, 1962), 245.

15. Daniel Steele, *A Defense of Christian Perfection* (New York: Hunt and Eaton, 1896), 110.

16. Corlett, *The Meaning of Holiness,* 112.

PART III

1. W. E. Sangster, *The Pure in Heart* (New York and Nashville: Abingdon Press, 1954), 60.

2. John Wesley, *The Letters of John Wesley,* ed. John Telford (London: Epworth Press, 1931), 5:223.

Appendix

1. Preamble of Constitution and Articles of Faith, *Manual,* 26-31.

Other Contributions by John A. Knight

Beacon Bible Commentary, Volume 9: Philippians
BF083-410-3087

Beacon Bible Expositions, Volume 9:
Philippians/Colossians/Philemon
BF083-410-3206

Beacon Dictionary of Theology
(contributor)
BF083-410-8119

Go . . . Preach
(with the Board of General Superintendents)
BF083-411-4283

The Holiness Pilgrimage: Developing a Life-style
That Reflects Christ
BF083-411-0997

In His Likeness: God's Plan for a Holy People
BF083-410-3664

What the Bible Says About Tongues-speaking
BF083-411-2671

Order from
Nazarene Publishing House
1-800-877-0700